BACKSTAGE AT THE PALACE

BACKSTAGE AT THE PALACE

AN IRREVERENT
ROMP
THROUGH
THE
HALLS OF JUSTICE

HENRY STEINBERG

Stoddart

First published in 1993 by
Stoddart Publishing Co. Limited
34 Lesmill Road
Toronto, Canada
M3B 2T6
(416) 445-3333

Canadian Cataloguing in Publication Data

Steinberg, Henry
Backstage at the palace

ISBN 0-7737-2690-X

1. Quebec (Province). Superior Court.
2. Justice, Administration of – Quebec (Province).
3. Conduct of court proceedings – Quebec (Province).
I. Title.

KEQ1082.S85 1993   347.714′035   C92-095639-4
KE345.S85 1993

Cover design by Brant Cowie/ArtPlus
Typesetting by Tony Gordon Ltd.
Printed and bound in Canada

This book was inspired by real people and true stories. Some incidents have been embellished with imaginary details, others have been altered or combined. The characters are composites, and most names and other identifying features have been changed to avoid even unintentional embarrassment.

Stoddart Publishing gratefully acknowledges the support of the Canada Council, Ontario Ministry of Culture and Communications, Ontario Arts Council and Ontario Publishing Centre in the development of writing and publishing in Canada.

To Janice
*who encourages me
to laugh at myself, and
to take humour seriously!*

Contents

Preface

I am a judge, an observer of the tragedy and comedy that unfold in the courtroom. I am the audience in the theatre where emotions are displayed, passions are vented, and eloquence is cultivated. I am the narrator of stories and author of judgments. I live and work in the Palais de Justice in Montreal.

Every courthouse has its theatres, where an exaggerated reflection of the world is presented and personal stories are performed. Each courtroom is a stage. Lawyers, parties, and witnesses make their appearances, enjoy one or more moments at centre stage, portray themselves, recount events, and contribute pieces to the jigsaw of a lawsuit. The proud and the humble, the clever and the simple, the learned and the illiterate, the concerned and the indifferent parade, testify, and plead before the court.

The judge controls with mind and directs with voice and gesture under constant scrutiny in the open courtroom. Each word is recorded, some are transcribed and published. The press, in its role as representative and reporter to the world, is ever vigilant and frequently critical. Always surrounded and seen, the judge is very much alone, guided by conscience, the oath of office, and a duty to the parties, society, and the law.

The judge must be a chameleon, able to adapt to constantly changing circumstances, with manner and expression that encompass the spectrum of human experience, ranging from humble servant to stern ruler, from parent and friend to distant observer, while remaining faithful to the facts and guiding legal principles.

When evidence and argument are completed, the cast of parties, attorneys, and witnesses reassembles, this time as the audience. The judge, no longer a passive spectator, becomes the actor who pronounces a monologue for the benefit of those present and some who are absent, seeking to harmonize substance and style for an audience at once intimate and distant. Judicial literature emerges from this stage, sometimes blemished and uneven, often ponderous and dull, but occasionally graceful, precise, and majestic.

Knowledge and openness are the hallmarks of a credible legal system, and guarantors of its fairness and effectiveness. Through personal memoir, seasoned by gentle humour and the occasional tart comment, I seek to lift some of the secrecy and admit fresh air backstage at the palace.

HENRY STEINBERG
Montreal, Quebec
September 1992

Acknowledgments

*B*ackstage at the Palace is the product of my interest in people and delight in language and storytelling. It could not have been written without the encouragement, generosity of spirit, and candour of many friends and colleagues. I acknowledge the particular assistance of Chief Justice Lawrence A. Poitras, and of Betty Drummond, Sandra Hausman, Michael A. Levine, Barbara Kay, Billy Mauer, Jan Whitford, and Kathryn Dean. Throughout I benefited from the constant involvement and honest criticism of my wife, Janice, who laughs, cries, and shares all precious experiences with me.

BACKSTAGE AT THE PALACE

I

Setting the Stage

1

The Palace

History and politics, geography and demography have endowed Montreal with a unique vocation. It is the metropolis of a Canadian province where English common law and French civil law co-exist and enrich each other. Civil law governs relations between private citizens. Its principles, transplanted from Napoleonic France, were incorporated in the Civil Code adopted in the mid-nineteenth century and subsequently amended and revised to reflect a vibrant, evolving society and changing circumstances. Public law, criminal law, and much commercial law are inspired by the traditions of English common law. The proximity of the United States is apparent, and the influences of American business culture and values make constant inroads.

This amalgam of legal systems is complicated by the use of two languages in the text of legislation and in testimony and pleadings before the courts. Criminal trials are conducted in the language of the accused and comments in the other language are translated. In civil cases, the witness speaks in the language of his or her choice; judges, attorneys,

3

and court personnel switch to that language with more or less proficiency. All lawyers and judges are presumed to comprehend and speak both English and French — though this is not always the case and errors are often ignored.

Through this interplay of languages, new words and expressions emerge that are unknown in either France or England but are perfectly comprehensible to those who live and practise law in the province of Quebec. This is especially apparent in the Palais de Justice in Montreal. The situation spawns brilliant bilingual puns and *jeux de mots*, occasional unintended insults and some linguistic confusion, but remarkably the process works, and works well, when lubricated with consideration and good humour.

In the French tradition, certain buildings are designated as *hôtels* and others as *palais*, or palaces. The Houses of Parliament are known as the Hôtel du Gouvernement, the city hall as the Hôtel de Ville, the Mint as the Hôtel des Monnaies. Buildings with loftier purposes, such as the sports arena, may be known as the Palais des Sports, the convention hall may be a Palais des Congrès, and every courthouse is a Palais de Justice.

Every courthouse is a "palace" regardless of its size, location, age, or importance. In the city of Quebec, the *palais* is a new building, whose majestic entrance hall and atrium feature large, exposed and highlighted ventilation ducts conceived in the tradition of Paris's "sixties modern" Centre Pompidou. The *palais* in Ste. Agathe, a town in the heart of the Laurentian Mountains north of Montreal, consists of three small rooms on the second floor above a bakery; the building formerly housed an auto parts dealer and garage.

The Trois-Rivières *palais* was built in the nineteenth century. In a futile attempt to modernize the facilities, the clothes cupboard in the judge's office was equipped with a toilet and sink. It is separated from the office by a folding fabric door that neither muffles noises nor obstructs the free circulation of odours. The heating system is so uneven that on a recent visit I was advised by my usher that several of my colleagues refused to sit when the temperature inside the courtroom falls below fifty degrees Fahrenheit.

On my first visit to the old Joliette *palais*, I presided in a courtroom that the judges affectionately call the "chicken coop," where the judge sits in a distant alcove, hidden behind a high enclosure. He is barely able to hear the arguments of counsel. Only his shoulders and head are visible to onlookers. The ventilation system is less than effective and air conditioning is nonexistent.

Justice Pierre Pinard recalls presiding in a criminal jury trial in Joliette on a stifling June day. On the morning of the first day, he ordered the court officials to provide an electric fan for ventilation. He repeated the order on the second day, but a fan could not be found. On the morning of the third day, he was hot, exhausted, and exasperated. When the order was repeated once again, the court clerk looked up and remarked, "*Monsieur le juge*, no one can see your body behind the enclosure. Why don't you adopt the practice of Mr. Justice X? Remove your pants and sit in your underwear!"

The St. Hyacinthe *palais* is a product of the sixties. Its grand hall is adorned with a magnificent sculptured mural by Jordi Bonet, depicting the major architectural features of the town. Regrettably, the judge's attention is distracted from its beauty by the collection of garbage pails randomly placed on the upper bookshelves of his private office to catch falling drops from a leaking roof.

My *palais* in Montreal is a seventeen-storey high-rise, built twenty years ago, fully equipped with cells, a parking garage, cafeteria, libraries, and twelve floors of offices and court-rooms connected by a labyrinth of public and private stair-ways, elevators, escalators, corridors, passages, and halls. The ceremonial entrance faces south onto Notre Dame Street, and the warren of small, crooked cobblestone streets that make up Old Montreal. The streets are flanked by squat, stone buildings, remnants of the past, originally built as homes and small shops and subsequently converted to factories and warehouses. In the last quarter-century they have been transformed into homes, boutiques, and restaurants. Beyond is the St. Lawrence River, the transportation corridor that spawned the city 350 years ago.

Notre Dame Street represents authority and permanence. It is the street of the City Hall, the Basilica, the old courthouse, and the Château de Ramezay, residence of the former governors of Canada. Tourists, strangers, and government dignitaries approach the palace from Notre Dame Street. They enter into the high-ceilinged public lobby and are confronted by a round information desk that sits amidst a forest of notice boards and directories announcing forthcoming marriages, the days' criminal trials, Worker's Compensation hearings, and the office numbers of judges, government services, and other personnel. To the right is La Caisse Populaire des Fonctionnaires de la Province de Québec, the Peoples Savings Bank for Government of Quebec Public Service Employees. The "Caisse Pop" is adjacent to the Marriage Celebration Room, a bare-walled secular chapel where civil marriages are performed. In the rear, escalators and elevators lead to the courtrooms and offices.

St. Antoine Street to the north is built on a former riverbed which lay outside the original walls of Old Montreal. It is a major traffic artery, the street of the underground Metro, the parking lots, the buses, and the exit from the expressway. A few small stores, pawn shops, simple restaurants, and modest flats remain from the past, but most have fallen to the wreckers' ball. In their place is a series of parking lots and a depressed expressway — a modern moat that guards the palace.

Every morning, the people of the city converge on the palace in successive waves. First the workers — a small army of guards, clerks, mechanics, cooks, vendors, and secretaries — scurry from buses and subway cars to strategically located time clocks. They hurry to punch their time cards, then stop for a leisurely cup of coffee purchased from the mobile canteens that grace the lower floors. Judges and senior public officials drive into the private garage and are whisked by private elevators to the upper floors of the palace, where they, too, can enjoy their morning coffee while reflecting upon the day's workload and the state of the world. Window-less blue buses enter the garage carrying the day's prisoners, who will be tried by jury or a judge alone. The garage is the domain of the privileged and the imprisoned. Others must park in the surrounding area.

At nine o'clock, the lawyers arrive by taxi at the St. Antoine entrance. They carry briefcases, some swollen with papers and books, others empty, carried to impress onlookers. They rush into the basement, where they shed their outer clothing and re-emerge wearing the black gowns that give them an air of erudition and ritual adherence, caped crusaders ready to defend their clients' interests. A few wear their gowns with distinction, even arrogance. Others are less awe-inspiring: soiled shirts, unsewn seams, and traces of yesterday's lunch detract from their image.

After nine, the rest of the world enters the palace. Lawyers, litigants, witnesses, and spectators mingle in the entrance hall, the marketplace of justice. They study the lists of the day's criminal trials and the month's marriages. The canteens are surrounded by hungry customers who have not eaten since breakfast.

The Caisse Pop refuses to open until ten, but its machines distribute money to those who feed them plastic cards. The line of customers extends for thirty feet to the entrance of the Marriage Celebration Room, where a bride and groom wait amongst the lawyers, bank customers, criminals, vendors, witnesses, and observers. It is the dawn of another day at court. Welcome to the palace!

2

No Man Is a Hero
to His Mother
or His Caterer

In the English common law tradition transplanted to North America there is no school for judges, nor is there a system of promotion from lower courts to higher ones. Judges are appointed from among the active members of the Bar, and the selection system combines professional assessment with political decision.

Much has been written and even more has been whispered in law offices, restaurants, public washrooms, and private corridors about this process. Editorialists, politicians, attorneys, and judges delight in gossiping about the qualities and opinions of prospective nominees and the reconciliation of the principle of judicial independence with the realities of politics and government.

The judge is born on the day of his appointment. He steps across the Bar of Justice, transformed from actor to observer, from contestant to determiner. The years of legal practice fade into obscurity, personal relationships alter, and public perception changes. The confidentiality and loyalty owed clients are supplanted by openness and the duty to private conscience and the law. At this moment of transition, competitive attitudes wither. The judge cannot win or lose; there is only right and wrong. Each judge of a court wields identical power and enjoys the same benefits and conditions as his "sisters" and "brothers." A short time later, dressed in the black and red robes of office, he or she appears before family and friends, old confrères, and new colleagues to publicly accept new responsibilities and to pledge the application of all talent and energy to the impartial administration of justice.

I was born a judge on July 5, 1985. The Chief Justice presided at the official presentation ceremony held the following September. As the hushed audience rose at the usher's booming command, more than sixty judges marched solemnly into the large courtroom reserved for ceremonial occasions. The Chief Justice welcomed the audience and invited my friend, former partner, and new colleague Justice Kenneth Mackay to present and introduce me formally.

This was a moment to reminisce. More than a quarter-century earlier, I had met Kenneth Mackay and Richard Holden in the modest offices where they had recently founded their own firm. We practised together for ten years, a happy association, through which each of us thrived, despite our different professional interests. Mackay had cultivated an insurance law practice while serving as a part-time Crown prosecutor. Holden's talents were most evident in bodily injury and professional liability cases. Although my early experience was varied, my principal interest lay in the field of commercial and real estate law. Over the years, the area of my activity intensified and shifted from the courthouse to the boardroom. When Mackay was appointed a justice of the Superior Court in 1969, our warm personal relationship continued, and thereafter, in our family, the expression "the judge" meant the Honourable Mr. Justice Kenneth Mackay.

I subsequently left the firm and participated in other legal associations. Although my work grew in value and importance, I never recaptured the warmth and excitement of those early years. But twenty-five years after our first meeting, I rejoined my old partner, "the judge." His voice resonated through the courtroom.

> Ours is a Court which has produced, and I may say, still produces judges who are able to and do fulfill the true judicial role. . . . These men, and there were and are many others, were men of integrity who believed fervently in the paramountcy of the law above all else and the maintenance of a respected judicial system. Not for them the now fashionable practice of indulging in semantic acrobatics and captious quibbles over fine points of law, invested with giving a reasonable interpretation to and applying laws adopted by the people's representatives to preserve the social structure of our country.

I looked out, identifying family, friends, and associates, officers and former heads of the Bar Association, and focused on my parents sitting proudly in the front row.

I had been visiting friends in Vermont when an aide to the Minister of Justice phoned to confirm my appointment to the Superior Court of Quebec. He requested that I remain silent until the news was released by the government's press office. The following morning my son called to congratulate me on my appointment and to chastize me because he'd heard the news on TV. No matter, the appointment was official and Mother must be told. I phoned to give her the news.

"Mother, it's Henry. I called to tell you that I have been appointed a judge."

"Why are you disappointed with the judge?"

"Mother, you misunderstood. I, me, I have been named a judge."

"What did Mackay do to make you disappointed?"

"Please listen. Mackay is in England and has nothing to do with this. Forget him. Now, I, me, Henry, I am now a judge."

Mother then responded with great aplomb, "I am so happy. When you were in kindergarten, I knew that you would be a judge!"

No further comment could restore my stature. In one sentence she had reduced me to a whimpering four-year-old child and reasserted her authority. My appointment was nothing special; it was as inevitable and natural as that of the seed that had grown into a green onion.

Not content with her kindergarten knockout blow, Mother continued, "Do you know that when you were a little boy, I would frequently say to your father, 'Jack, we are raising a judge.' Here, speak to your father. He will tell you I said so."

I do not wish to downplay my relationship with my father, but it would never occur to me to phone him. He had not forgiven Alexander Graham Bell for inventing this means of communication, which he considered an unwelcome intrusion to be used only by others when calling police and hospitals. I cannot recall my father having phoned me more than half a dozen times in the past fifty years.

My father had been a successful industrialist. For many years he was the major shareholder and chief financial officer of a company engaged in the manufacture of metal furniture and related products. Throughout, he had been plagued by those two horsemen of the business apocalypse: inventory and overhead. I am convinced that he encouraged me to embark on a career in law so as to spare me the agony of falling victim to these mounted nemeses. During the years of my studies, he would frequently remark, "Remember, a lawyer has no inventory. That's what I like about the law business."

On this occasion, he limited his comments to congratulations and the expression of his hopes for my success in this new career. However, every few months thereafter, he would take me aside and confide, "I always said that a lawyer has no inventory. Now that you're a judge, you have no overhead either." The horsemen had finally disappeared, and the apocalypse was postponed indefinitely.

Kenneth Mackay's introductory comments brought my thoughts back to the courtroom.

All this is to say that this court, of which I have been proud to have been a member for over sixteen years now, has, in the person of Mr. Justice Steinberg, added to its ranks another judge of great integrity, of sound legal knowledge, of devotion to the law, and possessing the quality of good sense which is so inaptly called common.

Overwhelmed by the moment and the inevitable apprehension that precedes a new start, I found reassurance and comfort in the way news of my appointment had been received two months before. The following Monday morning, my office phone had begun to ring. By noon, I was informed that I had been duly considered and approved at the Brown Derby Delicatessen, Snowdon Deli, the Nautilus Room at the "Y," the locker room and the cafeteria in the courthouse, at Moishe's Steak House, McDonald's, Woody's Bar, Schwartz's Montreal Hebrew Delicatessen, and the coffee shops in each of the three office buildings where I had practised. I heard from my doctor, dentist, and butcher, the neighbourhood newspaper, and numerous lawyers — including some with whom I had not been on speaking terms. Ultimately, I received what was tantamount to royal sanction when an old client — a caterer who organized and catered commercial celebrations such as the viewing of new automobiles, the opening of shopping centres and wedding receptions — phoned my office. His precise words of congratulation were: "I knew it! I knew it! I always said you would become a judge because you know how to look at the important matters and forget the side dishes. Henry, there is only one decision of this government with which I agree, and you are he!"

Kenneth Mackay was concluding the introduction.

> Colleagues and members of the bar, it is my pleasure and honour to present our new judge — the Honourable Mr. Justice Henry Steinberg.

For two months I had anticipated and prepared for this occasion. My brief speech had been written and corrected, revised and rewritten a dozen times. It was a heady moment as I stood poised between the past and future, recalling the profession I had left.

> My years at the bar have been years of adventure, challenge, and excitement, coupled with occasional disappointment and disillusionment. I have experienced the pleasures of success and suffered the loneliness of failure. But throughout, I enjoyed the friendship and loyalty and benefited from the counsel of my confrères. I continue to cherish these relationships. These are my memories and recollections. . . .
>
> Justice is the responsible and reasonable synthesis of authority and freedom, public interest and individual rights. Freedom unrestrained by law is anarchy, public interest that does not respect individual rights is tyranny. An independent judiciary, as guardian of the rule of law, safeguards and delimits the relationship between public interest and individual rights.

As the ceremony ended, the stern courtroom visages of my new colleagues had been miraculously transformed into

13

warm, welcoming smiles as they offered encouragement and advice.

"Here's a key to the private elevators. Don't lose it. You only receive one during your career on the bench. I'm lucky. I have several."

"Remember not to accumulate more than five files at one time. If I ever hear you have reserved judgment in more cases than you have fingers on your hand, you'll hear from me."

"Don't eat in the judges' dining room!"

"Eat in the judges' dining room!"

My old friend Justice Louis Tannenbaum came over and said, "Henry, I have some advice for you."

"Yes, Lou," I answered. I was green and could use all that was available.

"I like the way you look in your robes. You still have hair, and it's black. Take my advice. Go take a picture before you lose half your hair and the other half turns grey. It will be a nice memento for your family."

As usual, Justice Tannenbaum was both practical and correct. The following day, I contacted Barry, a fashion photographer, and made an appointment to be photographed in the attire that one colleague calls "full dress."

At Barry's loft-type studio I was led through cardboard building facades, background screens, and props, into the changing room equipped with a coffee machine, refrigerator, and counter full of dirty cups and plastic dishes.

A few moments later, I emerged wearing a white shirt, black vest, striped formal pants, and the black and red robes that looked like something Gilbert and Sullivan's Lord High Executioner would wear. In less than an hour, Barry took several hundred pictures of me wearing this garb.

One week later, after we had gone through the proofs, Barry presented me with a series of eight-by-ten photographs and a portrait the size of a small card table. That weekend, my wife and I took the large photograph to a framing store where the owner gazed intently at the portrait, the gowned profile, the black hair, the face (which showed a tinge of arrogance), and the magnificent black and red tones of the robes. "What a nice picture, sir," he said, looking up at me. "In which church do you sing?"

The framed portrait is truly grand. So grand that I am embarrassed to display it. It hangs in splendid isolation in my basement, arrogantly surveying the elementary and high school diplomas and certificates of my three children on the opposite wall. When the basement is used for large parties, it is banished to the rear of the small unfinished cold-storage room beneath the stairs. Perhaps some day, in the distant future, when I have lost my hair and gained stature, the portrait will be relocated to a more prominent location as a reminder of the past.

Not so the eight-by-ten photograph given to my mother. It reigns serenely in the den of her Florida condominium, proudly supervising the pictures of her eight grandchildren, greeting each guest to her home with dignity. The photograph is known as "my son, the judge" and enjoys much greater respect and acclaim than I do.

Undoubtedly, the portrait was instrumental in encouraging mother to consult me about a problem she was experiencing with her landlord. Drawing upon my years of experience at the Bar, as well as my few months as a Superior Court judge, I drafted a letter which was clear, simple, and complete. I presented my mother with a typed version for her signature. She signed the letter after very careful perusal but declined my offer to mail it for her. She wished to obtain a second opinion before committing herself. She showed the letter to her neighbour, a bankrupt builder, and mailed it only after he gave his okay.

Several years later when the magazine *Canadian Lawyer* conducted a survey of lawyers and courthouse personnel to determine who were the best judges in Canada, I was

pleasantly surprised to find my name followed by this thumb-
nail sketch: "Well respected, but tough. Steinberg's immediate grasp of issues delights litigators."

While many of my friends and colleagues congratulated
me, Mother, as usual, had the final word: "I don't like to read
these things about you in the newspapers. It means you have
no heart."

During the months following my appointment, I learned that
the very announcement creates a barrier with many friends
and acquaintances. It manifests itself at the first encounters
when the newly appointed judge is asked: "What should I call
you?" or "How are you addressed?" Not surprising questions,
since even in court the title and style of address can cause
confusion and occasional humour. Over the past five years, I
have been called "Your Worship," "Your Grace," "Your Em-
inence," "Mister Judge," and "Your Honour," in addition to
the proper designations.

The secretary-treasurer of the garage where my son services his automobile insists on referring to me in the garage,
in the automobile showroom, and in conversations and
correspondence with the automobile manufacturer as "His
Excellency."

On one occasion, I was introduced to a community service
group of which I had long been a member as "our in-house
judge" — which was at least a notch above being called an
"outhouse judge."

I was not the only judge whose title caused confusion.
Throughout the years, Harry Blumenstein and Benjamin
Robinson had been friends, colleagues at the bar, and golf
companions. Shortly after the appointment of Justice Robinson to the Superior Court, the two friends were in the locker
room at a local golf club, preparing for an afternoon on the
links. Harry Blumenstein was unaccustomed to the new
position of his old friend and golf partner, and slightly uneasy.

As they were dressing he inquired, "How should I address you?"

Mr. Justice Robinson responded with a twinkle in his eye, "Harry, when you are in court, you should use the usual form of address and call me 'Your Lordship' or 'Votre Seigneurie.' When we meet on the street or when talking to other lawyers, you should refer to me as 'Mr. Justice Robinson.' But, Harry, seeing as we are old friends, here in the locker room of the golf course, you can call me 'Judge'!"

A classic and frequently repeated story about one former justice concerns a French-speaking witness who had insisted on testifying in the English language. His vocabulary was adequate, but his accent and the occasional slip betrayed him. The witness had heard the attorneys refer to "Your Lordship" and sought to adopt this proper formal address. At the first appropriate moment, he addressed the presiding judge and with great courtesy called him "Your Lordshit." The judge, a man of great patience and understanding, smiled gently. The witness interpreted the smile as a sign of approval and continued to repeat "Your Lordshit" as a prefix to each answer. After four or five such occurrences, the smile turned to a wince. Finally, his patience exhausted, the judge turned toward the witness and said, "Why don't you just call me George?"

II

Backstage

3

Oyez, Oyez, All Rise!

In an earlier and perhaps more accommodating period, a newly appointed judge enjoyed the privilege of placing two family retainers on the public payroll. In this way, retired relatives or some who had never worked could be assured of stable employment and a pension. One of these retainers was appointed as the judge's crier or usher, the other as his court clerk.

The doings of these old-time ushers and clerks are legend. One senior colleague frequently regales his friends with stories of engaging his bank manager to act as his clerk. This selection was made because the manager had neat handwriting and could be relied upon to obtain the correct spelling of the name and address of each witness. Another colleague hired his chauffeur as an usher, and thereafter his car was washed daily and driven carefully at the public's expense.

The ushers and clerks depended on the judge's goodwill for their livelihood and security, which created a personal loyalty rivalling that of the feudal period. The judge, on the other hand, enjoyed the trappings of "Lordship." His usher and clerk were in constant attendance. His wish was their command. No judge would lift a book or carry a paper in public. The simple act of crossing a public corridor was imbued with pomp and ceremony. The judge, outfitted with striped pants, gown, and three-cornered hat, walked solemnly behind his usher, who swept his hands from side to side and bellowed, "Make a passage, make a passage!"

When the "new palace" was constructed in 1972, many of the old customs died. The layout of the building minimizes the number of public corridors crossed by the judges, and a network of rear passages and private elevators allows judges and courthouse personnel to move unseen between their private offices and the courtrooms.

The public purse could no longer support an army of private retainers, and the roles of the ushers and clerks changed. They ceased to be the private serfs of the judge and became employees of the administration, assigned to courtrooms only when courts are in session and their presence is required. Fortunately, a few oldtimers remain to reminisce and instruct new judges in the ways of justice.

I was appointed in the month of July, a period when only emergency and procedural matters are heard and the palace is relatively quiet. Nevertheless, the Chief Justice had asked me to sit for two weeks immediately following my appointment, and such requests are not denied.

Although I had practised as a lawyer for twenty-five years, I felt ill prepared for this new career. My introduction was limited to a hurried twenty-minute private ceremony in the office of the Chief Justice, where I had taken the oath of office in the presence of my son and wife the previous day.

"Get to work immediately," the Chief had said. "There will be plenty of time for parties and ceremonies in the fall."

I sat in my newly painted and furnished office on the seventh floor south, staring at the empty bookshelves, surrounded by the summer silence. Outside my window was an uninterrupted view of the air-conditioning apparatus. I wondered what momentous problems would be presented to me this first day. How would I handle a challenge to the legality of the Rental Board, an attack on the school curriculum for the following year, an injunction to clear Indian barricades, or even a contested custody dispute?

The shuffle of feet treading on the carpet could be heard. The door to my office was flung open, and a tall, lean, aging gentleman, an old-time usher, introduced himself: "My lord, I am Nantel. Follow me."

As we walked through the deserted corridor and descended in the judges' private elevator, Nantel explained that he had been in the employ of the government for many years. Before entering public service, he had been a policeman, a boxer, a merchant, and many other things. But he had missed his true vocation. He should have been a philosopher.

During the five-minute descent to the second floor, Nantel explained his philosophy of life and the intricacies of the public service union contract.

"My lord, the contract entitles the ushers to two coffee breaks each day. Remember to adjourn for at least fifteen minutes in the middle of the morning and afternoon sessions. If you respect my coffee breaks, I will take care of you and tell you what to do!"

At this moment, we had reached the second floor, where the corridor follows the northern perimeter of the palace and is lined with floor-to-ceiling windows. I gazed at the familiar neighbouring buildings: Jack's Musique, Cameras Simon, Simon's, Old Brewery Mission, and Taverne Herbe. My daydreaming was interrupted by Nantel's cough as he continued, "*Monsieur le juge*, I advise you never to think about the Court of Appeal. Remember, it takes three of them to make a single decision. You, you can decide alone."

My training as judge was now complete. Nantel thrust

open the rear door of the courtroom and bellowed with authority, "All rise!"

The court clerk rose smartly. The two attorneys shuffled to their feet. I entered gingerly, somewhat overwhelmed by the empty room and the small, raised platform where I was to sit.

"The Superior Court is now open. Mr. Justice Henry Steinberg is presiding! Be seated."

My career on the Bench had been launched. I was grateful that Nantel had pronounced my name correctly. In similar circumstances, my colleague Louis Tannenbaum had been introduced as "Mr. Justice Cannonball," Justice Irving Halperin had been confused with the manager of the Montreal Canadians hockey team and was presented as "Mr. Justice Irving . . . Grundman!" and Justice Benjamin Greenberg recalls being introduced as "Mr. Justice Benjamin Franklin." On later occasions I frequently was presented as "Justice Steinbergs" and "Justice Greenberg," but for this first court case, Nantel got it right.

The case was listed on the rolls of the practice court as an injunction. I was not required to decide important issues of the day and wield the awesome power of the law to halt an arbitrary act of government or correct some grave injustice. I was thrust into the midst of a neighbourly dispute. The complaints were less than momentous. The plaintiff sought a court order to restrain the defendant's son, who had leered at her lasciviously as if she were a prostitute. This ground dissolved when it was established that the young man in question was only twelve years old. The plaintiff further sought to prevent her neighbour's dog from messing on her lawn and barking at her guests.

Here is the cross-examination of the defendant:

Lawyer: Do you own a dog?

Witness: Yes.

Lawyer: What kind of dog?
Witness: A mongrel.
Lawyer: What breed?
Witness: The mongrel breed.

Some lawyers do not know when to be quiet and leave well enough alone. The plaintiff's attorney continued.

Lawyer: What do you call your dog when you're mad?
Witness: Must I answer that question?
The Court: Yes.
Witness: Asshole.

Later in the week, I was surprised to see my old friend Gerald Tremblay enter the courtroom and sit quietly in the farthest corner. Gerald is a first-rate trial lawyer who affects the air of a country bumpkin from Lac St. Jean, where he was born. He usually looks as though he should have visited the barber two weeks before and as often sports an unkempt moustache. One of his great gifts is a sense of humour, which he constantly displays as he confidently strides the narrow line between comedy and contempt. I pretended not to have noticed his entry.

The disputed issue was the finding of a labour arbitrator who had confirmed the plaintiff's dismissal for wearing improper attire and for poor grooming. His counsel quoted a case where a policeman had been fired for wearing his hair too long.

I interrupted his argument to observe, "The problem is not limited to policemen. I have known eminent lawyers who wear their hair too long . . . not to mention their moustaches."

For a moment the plaintiff's attorney was quiet, wondering whether I had intended to insult him. The silence was interrupted by guffaws from the rear of the courtroom, where Gerald was slapping his knees and bobbing his head. The attorney turned, and seeing Gerald convulsed with laughter, observed for the record, "I assume the Court was referring to the confrère Tremblay."

Confrère Tremblay left the courtroom with an elaborate bow.

Throughout the week, Nantel sat in the corner of the courtroom, a tall, slim Buddha, beaming approval, frowning disapprobation, and occasionally muttering under his breath according to his perception of the witness. Twice each day he would cough discreetly to remind me of the union contract and the designated coffee breaks. I reacted promptly to his coffee break interjections, though not to his other comments.

As the week drew to an end, the pace of work increased. By Friday morning, I had the distinct impression I was the only judge in the courthouse.

During the morning break, Nantel explained that in the summer months, experienced judges often referred files to their junior colleagues and went off to play golf on Friday afternoon. I told Nantel that although I was not a golfer, I owned a cottage in the Laurentian mountains north of Montreal, where I would like to spend the weekend tending garden and playing tennis. Nantel rose to his full height and said with a twinkle in his eye: "*Monsieur le juge*, you have been most correct and did not miss any of my coffee breaks. I shall tell you how to proceed. When we return to court, I shall stand near the door and will not allow anyone else to enter. If they bring more files I shall tell them that you are swamped with work and turn them away. At four o'clock stand up and announce, 'For administrative reasons the Court will adjourn until Monday morning,' then leave the courtroom and I will follow and lead you to your office."

I subsequently learned that Nantel had a surefire technique to discourage attorneys from presenting applications. He would stand at the door and insist that they allow him to read the proceedings before it was presented to the judge. When he reached the halfway point in his reading, a smile would begin to appear at the edges of his mouth. Three-quarters of the way through his reading, he would stare at the attorney and burst into laughter. At this point, most members of the bar, unable to restrain their uneasiness, would ask, "What's wrong?"

"This application . . ." he would reply with disdain, ". . . do you seriously think it will be granted? I know this judge. I have been sitting in the courtroom for the past week. You do not have a chance. Why, this morning alone, he refused two similar applications." He would give the lawyer a knowing wink and continue, "Today is Friday. I suggest you ask *Monsieur le juge* to postpone the application to Monday or Tuesday. Next week Mr. Justice — will be presiding in this room and you have a much better chance of succeeding before him."

The great fear of a new judge is that he may be doing the wrong thing and not know it. Few jobs are as lonely. The judge lacks the constant comment of clients and partners. This is most apparent during the first days. Perhaps it was this sense of loneliness that impelled me to drop by the office of the Chief Justice on Friday noon. To my surprise he greeted me with a broad grin and informed me that he had been hearing good things about my courtroom behaviour. I was puzzled. Never in my practice as a lawyer had I visited the Chief Justice to comment on the judges before whom I had pleaded. Nor could I imagine that the litigants in the mundane cases I had heard had done so. My bewilderment ended when the Chief's secretary explained that Nantel considered himself a connoisseur of judges, and every few days would drop by her office to comment on his charges. She, in turn, kept the Chief abreast of these comments.

I survived my first summer term under the watchful eye of Nantel.

The fall term begins in September. The palace offices are occupied, courtrooms come to life, and the corridors are filled with activity. Secretaries shuttle between their desks and the copying machines. Internal messengers push grocery carts full of files from office to office, and stray lawyers wander about in search of judges' offices, uncrowded washrooms, and exits. Some clerks and ushers mill about, waiting for the judge to appear. Others congregate near the water fountain, smoking, exchanging gossip, and filling water glasses and pitchers. The congestion backstage is increased by the presence of bicycle couriers wearing stretch pants, leather jackets, and crash helmets, who wander from office to office delivering urgent communications. Once the envelope is delivered, they reach for the portable phones dangling from their waists, announce the successful accomplishment of their mission, and request their next assignment.

Judges, resplendent in their red and black gowns, emerge from their offices and follow their ushers through the corridors to the private elevators and passages that take them to the courtrooms. Using the judges' private elevators has become a ritual imbued with an almost religious significance. The usher strides resolutely in the direction of the judges' elevator lobby totaly oblivious to the locked door controlling access. At the very last moment, he turns sharply towards the judge to request the key to this holy corridor. Inexperienced judges may fail to anticipate this unexpected pirouette and bump into their ushers, causing files and books to fall to the ground. The veteran magistrate reaches into his vest pocket, hands the key to his usher, and looks on calmly while the door is opened. Frequently, through the glass panels on either side of the door, one can detect the presence of other members of the judiciary awaiting the elevator's arrival. If they interrupt the ritual by reaching to open the locked door to the elevator lobby, an elevator will arrive and depart without them. On the other hand, should they step into the elevator and try to hold it until their colleague's usher manages to unlock the door to the lobby, obscene noises issue from within the elevator, which are not at all consistent with the dignity of their position. It is best not to interfere and risk angering the elevator.

Summoning the private elevators is not as easy as expected. Simple pressure on either the up or the down button is insufficient. These elevators will respond only if both buttons are pressed. I have not yet discovered whether this is a security device or a subtle architectural reminder to explore all avenues before embarking. The private elevator cab, tastefully decorated with the daily menu in the judges' private dining room, seems aware of its exalted role and ponders long before responding to the buttons pressed. As the cab travels, it gathers and distributes ushers and clerks, who carefully observe the rules of seniority and priority as they enter and leave on each floor.

To reduce elevator stress, I quickly adopted the practice of moving from one floor to another by the emergency stairway. Fortunately, my ushers do not find this extra activity contrary to the terms of the union contract. I have grown accustomed to the surprised looks of attorneys and witnesses when I emerge unexpectedly into the public corridor.

I had little occasion to see Nantel after the summer. However, he served as my usher on two subsequent occasions — each of which was noteworthy.

In the first case, a twenty-two-year-old man had angered his father's business partner. Unable to restrain himself, the partner had struck the young man in the face. He suffered a broken jaw and was unable to eat solids for a month, during which time his jaw was wired shut and he was nourished with liquids sipped through a straw. His marriage, which had been scheduled for the following week, was postponed, as was the honeymoon. After the wiring was removed, the victim was left with a residual permanent incapacity. He sued for loss of nuptial pleasures on the first night of his marriage, loss of salary while under medical attention, and for permanent incapacity.

The first heading of damages was dismissed when I discovered the fiancée was three months pregnant at the time of the incident. Nantel obviously disapproved of the victim's conduct and felt that he deserved the beating, albeit with less serious results. Throughout the plaintiff's testimony, Nantel frowned and breathed heavily. During the morning break, he looked at me and asked, "*Monsieur le juge*, what do you think?"

"I have not decided yet," I replied.

"*Monsieur le juge*," he continued, "I was a boxer in my youth. We boxers used to call that a 'bad lucky punch.'"

The last time I saw Nantel was during the Le Classy case. A lady of advanced years had gone to the Le Classy Club in the north end of Montreal to seek companionship. It was her lucky night. She met a gentleman of her vintage and they had spent a pleasant evening dancing and sipping Coca-Cola. At eleven o'clock in the evening, they had left the club and walked hand in hand along the icy sidewalks of Henri Julien Street. Suddenly, the woman slipped and fell to the ground. Her new friend fell on top of her and in the process, the woman broke her wrist. She sued the city of Montreal for having failed to maintain the street in a safe state and claimed $15,000 damages.

The city presented the usual defence: their records showed that the street was sanded and that the victim must have been careless and was responsible for the injuries suffered. Although the claim was less than solid I was favourably disposed towards the victim. I do not know if I was completely convinced of the merits of her suit, but after all, she was single, unfortunate, and elderly. I was overcome by the Robin Hood instinct and awarded her a sum, small enough that the city would be unlikely to appeal the judgment. The next day Nantel came to see me bright and early.

"*Monsieur le juge*," he said, "would you believe that I had the good fortune to leave the courthouse in the same elevator as that lady whose case you heard yesterday? She wasn't happy and said so to her lawyer. He told her he would file the appeal if she sent him a cheque for $1,000. But, *Monsieur le juge*, don't worry. I tapped her on the shoulder and said, 'Madam, the judge gave you a gift. You shouldn't throw away $1,000 on a useless appeal!'"

Other ushers did not possess the same cool confidence and knowledge. Once during the early days, I was assigned as an usher a young lady known to her friends as "the big brunette." On that particular occasion, I had been sitting in one of the large courtrooms usually used for commissions or tribunals of two or three members. The judge's platform and desk are extra long and there were two upholstered chairs on the platform behind the desk. During the morning break my usher asked, "Why do you think there are two chairs on the platform?"

"One for me and one for you," I replied with a wink.

About ten minutes after the hearing resumed, my eye wandered to the side and I observed "the big brunette" sitting on the seat beside me, her eyes peering intently at the lawyers. I managed to extricate her with great delicacy, and thereafter tried to remember my wife's admonition not to be satirical with strangers.

I am not the only judge to have overestimated an usher. When a distinguished defence attorney was appointed to the Bench, she was determined that her first jury trial be a model. In anticipation, she sent her usher to inspect the courtroom. He returned and informed her that all was ready and her presence was awaited. She followed her usher through the corridors with dignity and assurance. Upon arriving at the courtroom, she swept by her usher through the open door with gusto, only to find herself alone in the jury box. The usher had led her to the wrong door. She was obliged to beat a hasty retreat and re-enter the courtroom through the judges' entrance, with somewhat less gusto.

I recall when the government of Quebec invoked the override clause in the Constitution to reinstate a law banning English commercial signs that previously had been ruled unconstitutional by the Supreme Court. That day as I was walking through the back corridors of the palace, I was greeted by three or four clerks and ushers clustered around the drinking fountain. When one asked my opinion of this government act, I did not feel like getting involved in a long discussion and sought to avoid the subject with a jest. "I can understand how some French Canadians feel threatened by the very sight of an English sign. I feel threatened when I drive through Westmount and see all the addresses written in Arabic numerals." Then I continued down the hall.

Thereafter, for some unknown reason, one of the ushers who had been present on that occasion laughed whenever he met me. I did not think my comment had been that funny, but then people have different reactions to humour.

About a year later, I was standing in the corridor when the usher approached me, wearing his usual grin. "*Monsieur le juge*," he said, "do you remember you made the remark that you felt threatened by the Arabic numbers beside the doors in Westmount?" As I nodded he continued, "Well, the night after you made that comment, three of the ushers drove through Westmount to see if the addresses were really written in Arabic numerals."

Courthouse personnel tend to become cynical and even hardbitten as they hear myriad versions of the same story repeated frequently. Occasionally, however, a hearing takes an unexpected turn which startles even the most jaded. Such a moment occurred when a man was sued for divorce on the grounds that he had engaged in aberrant sexual practices. The mother-in-law testified that she had surprised him in the barn, having relations with a sheep. The matter might have ended there, but the French version of the idiom, "Let us return to business" or "Let's get down to brass tacks" is *"Revenons à nos moutons,"* which literally translates, "Let us return to our sheep." Jocelyne was my usher at the time of this bizarre testimony. Thereafter, whenever a lawyer suggested that we "return to our sheep," she could not contain her chortles. Attorneys and litigants would stare at her aghast. She and I understood.

For the past several years, Linda has been my assigned usher. She is a young, slight, blonde woman with large, blue eyes. She laughs at my jokes and generally keeps me informed of what transpires in the public corridors of the palace.

Linda was present when an attorney pleading a shareholder dispute in French seemed to be groping for the precise word to describe his client's predicament. Finally, his eyes lit up and he exclaimed, *"C'était un* 'deadlock.'" I leaned forward, looked over my glasses, and observed, "In English, we call that an 'impasse.'"

I spent a day and a half hearing this application to wind up a solvent company. Just before the lunch recess, I commented that the application must either be maintained or dismissed, and in both cases the shareholders would suffer. If I maintained the application, a solvent company would be wound up to their joint loss. On the other hand, if I dismissed the application, there was every likelihood that the contest and difficulties would continue, the parties would devote resources and energy to the dipute and once again, the company would suffer and decline in value to their joint detriment. Under the circumstances, I suggested that the parties make a final attempt to settle the problem on an amicable basis during the lunch recess.

At two-fifteen that afternoon, the attorneys asked Linda to inform me that their discussions were continuing and requested that I delay my re-entry into the courtroom. At three o'clock in the afternoon, I was informed that my presence was requested and that a settlement had been negotiated.

When I entered the courtroom, the attorneys stood and announced the successful conclusion of their negotiations. Following my usual practice on these occasions, I commended the parties and their attorneys. One of the parties, overwhelmed by the occasion, or perhaps the outcome of the settlement discussions, repeated loudly, "Thank you, thank you, Your Honour."

He then bounded up on the platform and grabbed and shook my hand. As I recovered from this unexpected gesture, he turned to Linda and said, "And you, you have the most beautiful blue eyes!"

Linda and I beat a hasty retreat from the courtroom. She fluttered her beautiful, blue eyes at me for the rest of the week.

4

Supporting the Judiciary

In recognition of the complexity of modern life and to ensure the serenity and efficiency of the judiciary, the government has established a department within the palace that bears the awesome title, Judicial Support Services. A small team of administrators devote their full attention to the welfare and service of the judiciary. Gone are the woes and cares of the private practice of law. All details of office equipment, repairs, stationery, broken telephones, personnel, and other housekeeping matters can be referred to them.

In the summer of 1985, business flourished, jobs were plentiful, and bilingual legal secretaries were scarce. It was not surprising that Judicial Support Services had difficulty finding a suitable secretary for me. The security and salary of the public service are unattractive during good times.

At first I managed without permanent help, but when September arrived, it became obvious I would have to take matters into my own hands.

"Find anyone you like," the manager of Judicial Support Services advised. "If she is willing to accept the salary and working conditions, we will hire her. The union will file a grievance, but that should not be a problem, because we are having trouble filling the two other open positions. Just don't spend money on agencies or advertisements. The year's budget is already allocated."

The following morning, I was walking along Cedar Avenue lost in my thoughts and oblivious to the sounds of car tires and brakes. In the distance, I noticed Justice Benjamin Greenberg pulling on the leash of the yappy bundle of hair that he calls a dog. Perhaps Ben would have an idea for me.

I have been walking and using public transportation to go to my office for many years. Two or three times weekly, a friend, former client, or professional associate stops and gives me a lift. At the very moment that I was planning to overtake Justice Greenberg, a red Corvette drew up beside me and the passenger door opened. I got in without hesitating and took the seat beside an attorney I had been associated with years earlier.

"Morning, Henry," he greeted me. "Let me give you a lift downtown."

"Oh, thanks, Aubry. How are you? It's been a while since you picked me up."

"Good, thanks. How about you? Now that you're a judge, I guess you don't have any problems of your own — only other people's problems?"

"Not quite," I answered. "As a matter of fact, I do have a problem. Maybe you can help. I need a top-flight bilingual legal secretary who is prepared to accept less than the going salary in exchange for security and a reasonable life. Any ideas?"

"For you?" he asked.

"Uh-huh."

"Paul's old secretary, Jacqueline, may be available. You

remember her from the days we were together? Apparently she got fed up with the pressure and quit. For the last few years she's been freelancing from her home doing translations. She may be ready for a full-time job. I'll call you later and give you her phone number," he added.

"Good."

We continued talking about mutual acquaintances. The car leaned around the corner onto St. Antoine Street and continued to the palace. As usual, the driveway in front of the building was narrowed to one lane, cars were backed up at the garage door, the taxi stand was overcrowded, and the excess cars had spilled onto the second traffic lane of St. Antoine Street. Aubry left me off in the middle of the congestion and the car lept forward towards the expressway.

I had not seen Jacqueline for thirteen years, but I remembered her well. Her intelligence and skills were exceptional. The young lawyers in Paul's office had consulted her frequently. It was rumoured that many clients preferred her legal opinions to those of some members of the firm. Paul had urged her to attend law school and offered to finance her studies, but without success. She had preferred to remain a legal secretary, a job for which she was overqualified.

Jacqueline exhibited contradictory personality traits. She could be tough and efficient, almost brutal. At other times, she would drift off and withdraw into herself. She dressed with artistic flair and professed to write poetry when she was home alone. She had absorbed some of the idealism of the sixties and the disillusionment of the seventies. She could be sensitive, trusting, and vulnerable, but then the mask would return and she would be detached, professional, cynical, and sarcastic.

I did not imagine that she would accept a position in the palace, but if she did, life would never be the same again. She would assert her personality and challenge and taunt me. If she disagreed, I would have to convince and cajole her into doing things my way. But I would have one sure friend in the palace. Even more importantly, no judgment or even letter would leave my office if it failed to meet her standards. The palace is replete with respectfully compliant public servants, attentive lawyers, admiring audiences, and polite litigants. She would be a welcome antidote and would add a touch of realism in this theatrical world.

I reached for the phone.

"Jackie, it's Henry," I announced.

"I've been expecting your call. I spoke to Aubry," she responded.

"Will you take a position in the public service for half of what you're worth?"

"I'm willing to try. You know I haven't held a steady job these last few years. I've been working at home doing translations. It's been more than ten years since I last saw you. What if we don't get along?"

"Jackie, I need you now while I make the transition from lawyer to judge. Anytime you're not happy, you can quit and go back to freelancing."

"When do you want me to start?" she asked.

"This afternoon," I replied.

"*Attends!* Wait a minute. I'll start tomorrow and I'm not promising to stay. I'll work only as long as I wish."

"I know. It's a deal!"

"*Au revoir, Monsieur le juge.*"

"Bye."

Jackie joined the public service the next morning. She settled in as if she were returning to a familiar habitat after a brief absence. For several months she and I adjusted to each other's habits. Life was uneventful.

In the spring following my appointment to the Bench, my secretary's typewriter became ill. This occurrence was not surprising, because typewriters, like offices and other benefits to judges, are allocated on the basis of seniority. Judges appointed twenty years ago have the finest offices, march at the head of official processions, sit in the front rows, make the first selection of assignments and holidays, attend the best conventions, and get the newest typewriters. As I was a novice, my secretary only rated a six-year-old IBM machine. When I asked Judicial Support Services to provide a new machine for her, I was informed that the delay for new typewriters for secretaries of judges of my vintage was between three and four years.

At first, the problem was bearable. Few attorneys and litigants noticed the extra blanks following certain letters, and the uneven space between lines did not result in any miscarriage of justice. My secretary and the typewriter hobbled along. But in April the thing expired. Maintenance men and mechanics applied their skills to no avail. The typewriter could not be resuscitated. Fortunately, the colleague with whom I shared quarters in the palace had had the foresight to introduce a typewriter from his former law office to the public service, so on some occasions, my secretary had access to this machine. At other times, typewriters were borrowed from the maintenance department and from other judges on the floor whose secretaries were ill or on vacation.

Obviously, the situation could not continue as it was. I considered a direct appeal to the Chief Justice, but he was preoccupied with other matters. The Minister of Justice had decided to reduce the number of personnel available to the court by eliminating most of the ushers and half the secretaries — a move that the Chief was fighting valiantly. He repulsed all initiatives by the Minister and ultimately earned a place in legal history by launching a lawsuit against the Minister of Justice and seeking an injunction to restrain implementation of threatened staff cutbacks. I would have to solve the typewriter problem alone.

"You think you can solve all problems with charm and a smile," my secretary taunted me. "This time only money or a good mechanic will succeed, and judges are not usually well equipped in either of those departments. You could dye your hair grey and try to fool the people in Judicial Support Services into thinking you've been around for years. Ha! Ha! If you pull out your teeth and walk with a limp they may even give you a computer!"

"Don't despair, I shall take this matter up with the Minister of Justice personally. Your new typewriter is as good as ordered," I muttered as I left the office. Just the same, I was not entirely sure that a meeting with the Minister would do a lot of good. I had met him a year earlier when we had participated in the roast of a common acquaintance, but our relationship was casual.

During the following month I reflected upon the problem of the typewriter in my spare time but was unable to develop a plan of action. The propitious moment arrived unexpectedly. My wife and I were attending a lecture at the Law Faculty of McGill University, and the Minister was one of the scheduled speakers. At the cocktail reception following the lecture, I waved in his direction. He approached me and began speaking, "Can you believe that the Chief Justice is actually sueing me because I want to reduce the secretarial staff? I know that judges need secretaries but surely they don't need a private secretary at all times. What do you think?"

"Mr. Minister," I replied, "the problem is easy and soluble. All that's necessary is to add one word to the law and you can eliminate all the secretaries."

"How?" he asked with a puzzled look.

"It's simple and cheap," I continued. "The Code of Procedure says that 'the judge shall give reasons for his judgment.' Just add the word 'not,' so it reads, 'The judge shall not give reasons for his judgment,' and your problem is solved."

"Be serious, the roast was last month," he admonished me. "Tell me about your personal situation. Can you manage to get by with a secretary two and a half days a week?"

"Speaking personally," I said, "I can get by easily with a secretary zero days a week. For me to have a secretary is a complete and absolute waste of time."

"Why do you say that?"

I thrust home the sword. "Because her typewriter is broken. My secretary has been unable to type anything for a month, and I'm too junior to merit one of those new Olivettis your Ministry is supplying to judges with five years or more of seniority."

At that point my wife and the wife of the Minister joined us, and we discussed the evening's lecture. Although I was convinced that I had made my point and all would be solved, I did not respond to my secretary's taunt the following day.

"Well, did you see your friend, the Minister of Justice? Did you tell him about the typewriter that refuses to type? Will you invite him to the typewriter's funeral?"

"I've an important case to hear today and I've no time to worry about typewriters," I answered as I disappeared into my private office.

That week two representatives of the Department of Justice accompanied by a representative of Judicial Support Services appeared at my office to inspect the typewriter.

"They came to see the typewriter today," my secretary informed me. "That's the way they work. If you complain, they investigate and send reports, but nothing happens. Why don't you speak to the Chief Justice? Are you afraid?"

"The problem will be solved," I assured her. "Have faith in the administration."

"The administration, the administration, I wonder if they can type a judgment on a dead typewriter."

The ringing phone interrupted her tirade.

That July I underwent surgery. While I was lying in the hospital recuperating, the phone in my room rang and my wife answered. It was my secretary announcing that a new typewriter had been delivered to the office that day.

"My husband spoke to the Minister," my wife responded. I must have dozed off at that moment — I have no further recollection of the conversation.

When I returned to the office in early September, my secretary was preening like the owner of a new automobile. "Did you really speak to the Minister?"

"Of course."

"Are you trying to tell me that he has nothing better to do than to worry about my typewriter?"

"Yes."

"Don't you realize that he is responsible for hundreds of laws, thousands, tens of thousands of prosecutions, twenty or thirty courthouses, and twenty-three thousand employees, and is defending a suit brought against him by the Chief Justice? And do you think he is worrying about my type-writer? They must have made a mistake in the storeroom. They probably confused you with Justice Greenberg. He's been here for at least ten years. That's it."

"No," I replied. "The Minister has his priorities. He knows how much the typewriter means to you."

"Huh!" she muttered and shrugged her shoulders. "You think everyone is worried about you."

The official opening of the courts takes place on the first Wednesday following Labour Day. In Montreal, the formal ceremonies are attended by judges, lawyers, Bar officials, and special visitors from England, France, and the United States — as well as the federal and provincial Ministers of Justice. Lawyers celebrating their fiftieth anniversary at the Bar are honoured. The Chief Justice and government ministers frequently use the occasion to announce new policies and initiatives because they are sure the press will attend. At the entrance to the large hall where the ceremony is held, I brushed against the Minister of Justice.

"How does your secretary like her new typewriter?" he asked.

"Just fine, Mr. Minister," I smiled.

We entered the hall together.

It should be self-evident that judges express their thoughts in writing as well as orally and that the drafting of a serious judgment requires substantial editing and revision. The essential reference books are the Civil Code, the Criminal Code, and a good dictionary — so I was not surprised when my secretary asked me to help her obtain a *Petit Robert* — one of the standard French dictionaries.

"Write a letter to Judicial Support Services," I advised. "Better still, write in my name and mention the fact that it is necessary for your work. And don't make the letter too polite," I added.

"Sure, sure," she responded. "I wonder if they have any money left in the budget. After all, this is October and the fiscal year ends in March."

"Write the letter and see what happens," I repeated as I left the office.

The letter was drafted, signed, and delivered that very afternoon.

When I entered the next morning my secretary had a scowl on her face. "They phoned to say I cannot have a *Petit Robert* because it costs $51. They offered me an *Illustrated Larousse*, which costs only $37. It is all the government can afford. What do I do now?"

"Phone back immediately and tell them I use words and not pictures to explain my decisions. I am a judge, not a cartoonist. If that doesn't work, ask if I can add $14 to the cost of the *Larousse* and buy the *Petit Robert*. Tell them that Judicial Support Services and I will jointly own the dictionary in the proportions of two-thirds and one-third. If they refuse that offer, take the *Larousse* because you must never say no to gifts from the administration."

Our various tactics failed to sway the authorities. My

secretary received the *Illustrated Larousse*. For a brief period I considered offering it to a local bookstore as a down payment on a *Petit Robert*, but Judicial Support Services must have anticipated my larcenous thoughts. They had arranged for someone to work overtime and stamp the words "Property of the Department of Justice" on every tenth page of the dictionary.

When my secretary's birthday rolled around I purchased and presented her with a *Petit Robert*. Now, while she types and corrects my judgments, I study the pictures in her *Larousse*.

The Chief Justice has a special budget for the acquisition of books by the members of the court and an elaborate system to ensure the equitable distribution and proper utilization of those funds. Each year, a comprehensive list of available books is compiled. Each book is assigned a number of points, which bear a relationship to the price of the book. A book with a value of $10 is assigned one point, a book with a value of $20 is assigned two points, and so on. The completed list, which is about twenty pages long, is distributed to all the judges of the court, and they are invited to make their selections. Each judge is permitted to order books with a total value of thirty points.

When the list arrives in my office, I am always overcome by the impulse to test the system. Invariably, I order books whose numerical value adds up to thirty-one points. I take particular care to include in the two-point category one book that is of no particular interest to me. For three years this excess went unnoticed by Judicial Support Services, which administers the program. Presumably other colleagues were less avaricious or mischievous. Perhaps the people who controlled the distribution of books were generous, lazy, or both. It mattered not. I had triumphed. Judicial Support Services was fallible. The system could be beaten, and I had won for three consecutive years.

Alas, this year I was found out. Two weeks after I made my selection, my secretary grinned at me and announced: "Ms. Queenie Davis, the third assistant-secretary of Judicial Support Services phoned this morning. She said there's some irregularity in your book order. And don't ask me to call her back, because I won't. We both know why she's calling. This is one problem you'll have to solve for yourself." She thrust a piece of paper under my eyes and continued, "Here's her telephone local."

"All right, all right," I replied. "If you can't handle the situation, I'll call her personally."

"When?" I could hear the impatience in her voice.

"When I'm good and ready. Haven't you a judgment to type or a paper to file?"

"Just make sure you call her in my presence. I want to hear you wiggle out of this one."

"You will and I shall."

All morning I regretted my bravado. I could plead innocent error and agree to the removal of that book of cartoons about lawyers from the list, but I would lose face in front of my secretary. There are no problems, only solutions. One would present itself.

At noontime I sat in the cafeteria eating a sandwich and reflecting upon my plight. Various solutions passed through my mind. I had never met Ms. Queenie Davis. Was she susceptible to my charms? Would she be tempted by an arrangement of flowers? Could I convince her that her arithmetic was wrong? Would she allow me to use one of next year's points?

"Can I join you?"

I looked up and nodded to my colleague, Justice Mass, who approached the table. His tray was loaded with the daily special. Obviously, he did not have to struggle with problems of books, points, and morality.

As we ate, I asked him if he had completed his book order.

"Yes."

"Did you manage to select books that added up to precisely thirty points?"

"As a matter of fact," he replied, "I think the total is only twenty-nine."

Lights flashed and bells rang in my head. Salvation was at hand.

"Lend me a point," I begged.

"Sure, as a matter of fact, you can keep it. But what do I do?"

"Nothing. Just come up to my office after lunch, and I'll attend to everything."

At precisely two o'clock I returned to my office. Justice Mass followed closely. I glanced at my secretary with a triumphant air and commanded, "Get me that civil servant at Judicial Support Services who has the book problem! And come into my office so you can hear the conversation on the speaker phone."

A minute later I was seated at my desk, facing my secretary and Justice Mass while I spoke to Queenie Davis.

"Yes, Ms. Davis. I understand you have a problem."

"Oh, nothing serious, *Monsieur le juge*, just a slight irregularity in your book order."

"What irregularity?" I asked innocently.

"You have ordered books with a total value of thirty-one points."

"Is that a problem?"

"Yes, yes. We have a very strict budget. The government is clamping down and we were instructed to check every order carefully. Surely you have heard of the budgetary restrictions in the Department of Justice."

"There was something in the newspaper. But does the Minister of Justice worry about one extra point?"

"A penny saved is a penny earned. We must be careful at all times. This is taxpayers' money."

"What do you suggest, Ms. Davis?"

"I have no suggestions. I must remove a book from your order. Which one do you want removed?"

"Wait a moment. I have a suggestion. I have a solution. I have just acquired one point from my colleague, Mass. Please check his list and you will see that he ordered books for only twenty-nine points. I borrowed one of his points. The budget is now balanced. The government is saved, and you can send me the book."

"*Non, Monsieur le juge.*"

"No? Do you question my word? Mr. Justice Mass is sitting in front of me and will confirm this personally."

"*Monsieur le juge*, I do not doubt the truth of what you say, but our computer is not programmed to make trades and exchanges among judges. There is no alternative. I feel sorry for you and understand that you may think we are acting unfairly, but I must ask which book you want removed from your order."

My secretary made a grimace. She obviously sensed my discomfort and was waiting to witness my humiliation. Mass looked at me as if I had taken leave of my senses. Only now did he realize the full scope of the nefarious scheme in which I sought to embroil him.

"Ms. Davis, you are undoubtedly correct. The rules of the Department of Justice must be respected. The budget must balance both on an individual basis and on a collective basis."

"Thank you. Which book shall I remove from the list?"

"Ms. Davis, in the presence of my secretary and my colleague Justice Mass, I, Henry Steinberg, Justice of the Superior Court, authorize you to remove from my book order the book of cartoons about lawyers having a total point count of two."

"Thank you, *Monsieur le juge*. Goodbye."

"No, one minute Ms. Davis. Your books are still not in balance."

"How so?"

"Ms. Davis, I now have ordered only twenty-nine points. Also Mr. Justice Mass has ordered only twenty-nine points. What will you tell the Department of Justice? How will you balance your budget?"

"It is not serious. We will think of an answer," she said with a chuckle.

"Ms. Davis," I continued, "now I shall propose a solution to balance your points. I want you to take my leftover point and the leftover point of Justice Mass and buy yourself that book of English cartoons as a gift from Justice Mass and myself. When you have finished the book, please tear it in two, and send one half to my colleague Mass and one half to me."

Ms. Davis broke into an honest and full laugh.

"*Monsieur le juge*, you will receive your cartoon book. But remember, next year, do not exceed your allocation. The Minister and the Chief Justice will not be happy."

"Ms. Davis, next year we shall worry about next year. In the meantime, I give you my word that I shall lend the cartoon book to Justice Mass so that he can read it as well. *Bonjour!*"

It would be wrong to give the impression that life in the palace is characterized by deprivation, shortages, and inadequate facilities. In certain areas, generosity abounds. We live, for example, in a lush jungle of elastic bands. Every file is held tightly closed by two to five colourful rubber bands. The stationery supply room bursts with these expansive treasures, and the drawers of my desk are crammed with them. To survive this thriving rubber underbrush, I have adopted the practice of rating files by the number of elastic bands. Each file that leaves my office is embraced by a number of elastic bands that corresponds to its level of difficulty. Major constitutional problems merit five rubber bands; murder cases receive four, as do substantial shareholder disputes. The average divorce will enjoy a two or three rating, and disputes between neighbours must get by with one meagre band. Having successfully installed this system, I now propose to rate the lawyers in the file by the colour of the elastic bands. Within a year or two, the complete system will be in effect, and a judge will be able to establish the difficulty of a file and the ambiance of the courtroom by a glance at the colour-coded elastics. Ultimately this system will be offered to courthouses throughout North America.

The courtrooms are also awash in a sea of Liquid Paper — the pasty white fluid that comes in an infinite variety of small bottles. When it is dabbed onto typed, handwritten, or photocopied inscriptions, it leaves a telltale white blob that obliterates the writing and adheres to the preceding page like flypaper. Liquid Paper allows court clerks to correct minor errors and makes the court record look like a relief map of the Arctic.

We also enjoy a surfeit of ashtrays, although smoking is discouraged in public areas. The palace doors are guarded by heavy, cylindrical, free-standing, two-foot ashtrays. They are used as door stops, and their containers overflow with foam coffee cups, chewing gum, and unused elastic bands. The ashtrays are accompanied by recycling containers containing the wads of paper that should never have been distributed in the first place.

Each floor in the palace has two magic boxes — one on the north side and one on the south side. The magic box is a rectangular wooden open-top box that sits on the corner of desks placed at the entrance to the private areas to control the flow of visitors. If you don't know what to do with a file, if you wish to dispose of unwanted papers that look too important to be recycled, or if you want to mail a letter or use the internal messenger service, you drop them into the magic box. Throughout the day, court ushers push grocery carts through the rear corridors, empty the contents of these boxes into the carts, and disappear into a special reserved elevator. Most of the papers are taken to their appropriate resting places. Some are mailed. Others vanish forever.

To the surprise of no one in the palace and everyone in the Ministry of Justice, the Chief Justice won the first round of his fight with the Minister of Justice. One of my colleagues issued a well-documented and scholarly judgment ordering the government not to implement the threatened cutback of secretaries and other court personnel. By law, such orders must be served upon a representative of the government. Remarkably, that day the senior justice officers could not be found. Their reserved parking spots in the garage were unoccupied, their telephone calls were forwarded to a central switchboard operator who was unaware of their whereabouts, and their office doors were locked. Concern spread about the palace that somehow the government might circumvent the court order by effecting the cutbacks before the judgment was served.

Only Queenie Davis, the third assistant secretary of Judicial Support Services and the person in charge of the acquisition of books and other printed materials for judges lingered in the building. Queenie had been counting her inventory and balancing her points when her department head declared a sudden and unexpected half-holiday. She wondered where everyone had gone that afternoon and presumed that it was something that did not concern her. Well, it didn't, until she answered the ringing telephone and heard the Chief's secretary order her not to leave the Judicial Support Services offices until the bailiff had served her with the injunction issued that morning to prevent the expected cutbacks.

Queenie now understood why she was the only person in the Judicial Support Services offices. She stood by the door, her ample body trembling, as she awaited the bailiff's arrival.

"Queenie," I called, as I walked by the door on my way to the private elevator, "what are you doing alone in the corridor? You should be careful. You might be mugged by one of those bicycle couriers."

"Oh, *Monsieur le juge*, do not make fun of me today. One of your colleagues has just issued an injunction against the Minister of Justice and I must receive the judgment in the name of the Minister. If I do so, I shall be in trouble with all the people in Judicial Support Services and the Department of Justice, and if I hide and disobey the order of the Chief Justice to remain, I could end up in jail."

"Queenie, do not be afraid," I said. "You have friends among the judiciary. Do you think I have forgotten that you gave me an extra point when the Minister was not looking? Would I forget your concern over my broken typewriter? Here, allow me to give you a hard candy. Pull yourself together. The Chief and all the judges know what a wonderful job you are doing for Judicial Support Services. You just accept the injunction from the bailiff and give it to one of your many bosses. Should any of them bother you, march right up to my office and I shall give you another candy and issue an injunction of my own ordering them to cease molesting, harassing, or otherwise interfering with the best third assistant secretary in Judicial Support Services."

Ms. Queenie Davis smiled and kissed my cheek lightly. No harm came to her or to the secretaries and other personnel of the Court. As for the Minister of Justice, well, he ultimately resigned, was appointed as a Justice of the Superior Court, and at his presentation, formally apologized to his new colleagues on the Bench, admitted the error of his ways, and now advocates maintaining the full complement of court personnel. Regrettably, his successor, the new Minister, has yet to see the light and continues to advocate reductions in personnel and budgets.

When court is in session, the working hours of the judge are rigid. He sits from 9:30 to 4:30, with a break for lunch. Lawyers frequently use the lunch hour to review testimony, negotiate settlements, and prepare arguments. It is a convenient time for a judge to check a point of law or review his notes. In the more difficult divisions, the judge sits for two weeks each month and devotes the remaining two weeks to the writing of judgments and the study of files where judgment has been reserved. During those judgment-writing weeks, the judge may choose to work in his office, at the library, or elsewhere.

My social and inquisitive nature makes it difficult for me to write judgments in my office. The phone and the open door are irresistible distractions. My best writing is done at our cottage in the Laurentians, early in the morning, when the world sleeps and only the birds interrupt the silence.

On one occasion, I had been working at the cottage for a week and had prepared two draft judgments for typing by my secretary. I came down to Montreal Sunday night, intending to bring my work into the office and review the week's mail the next morning. Unaccustomed to the city sounds after a week in the mountains, I awoke early and was unable to fall asleep again. I rose at six o'clock in the morning and went to my office in the palace.

By ten to nine, I had completed my work. I spread the draft judgments on my secretary's desk and made a cup of coffee, which I sipped slowly while awaiting her nine o'clock arrival. When she didn't come in by nine-fifteen, I called her house.

"How are you feeling? I see you are still home."

"I was not well last night and I overslept," she replied.

"That's too bad. I woke up early this morning and I was in the office by 6:30. I reviewed the mail, laid out my draft judgments on your desk, and then had a cup of coffee while I waited for you. And you, you overslept!"

Her response was both quick and lethal.

"And I suppose you also left me your dirty coffee cup to clean!"

Time marched on relentlessly. My "new" typewriter was soon obsolete. The age of the computer had arrived, and once again my secretary taunted me.

"All the other secretaries on the floor have computers. Their judges don't sit around waiting for Judicial Support Services to have the budget available. Their judges pay for their secretaries' computers out of their pockets. They used their federal allowances for this purpose and don't squander their money on fancy dark suits and striped pants."

"Relax," I said, "have faith in the government. Common sense will prevail."

"When?" she asked. "You can't even contact your friend, the Minister. He's been appointed a judge. Do you know what he did? He took the computer from the Minister's office and had it installed in his office in the courthouse. His successor couldn't care less about you and your secretary. If I earned your salary and you earned my salary, I would buy you a computer."

"Your generosity is appreciated, but I have an idea. I shall write the Chief Justice and request a computer."

"Here we go again. Don't you realize that computers are distributed on the basis of seniority? Write all you want, you will have to wait years."

Realizing she was right, I decided to involve in my plans a colleague whose office adjoins mine. I prepared a special doubleheaded letterhead which featured both our names for the following letter to the Chief.

Joint Petition

Dear Chief:

The undersigned judges of the Superior Court humbly request that a microcomputer be made available in their offices to assure greater efficiency and better quality judgments.

Insofar as seniority and merit are concerned, they remind you that, taken together, they are 116 years old, have served for thirteen years, and continue to perform the work of two judges, twenty-four months a year, forty-eight hours daily.

Respectfully submitted,

I.J.H.J.S.C.   H.M.S.J.S.C.

The response was immediate.

Dear Colleagues:

I have this day referred your Joint Petition to the Treasury Board. Undoubtedly, the combined impact of your seniority and extended high-quality services will stir the members of the Treasury Board to loosen the strings of the purse containing the funds intended for the purchase of microcomputers for you and other deserving colleagues.

In the meantime, I invite you to exercise patience and consider petitioning the Almighty.

Your colleague,

THE CHIEF

Later in the month I met the Chief at a Christmas party. He assured me that the Treasury Board would act upon my request before the turn of the century.

5

Maintaining the Palace

The high volume of transient visitors and the nature of courthouse activities make security a particular problem at the palace. For better or for worse, I have never studied the various arrangements that have been made to safeguard the judges, witnesses, and palace occupants — but I have observed certain obvious measures.

First, there are frequent bomb threats. What easier way is there for the cowardly and disgruntled to disrupt court proceedings than to make an anonymous phone call and announce that there is a bomb concealed on a particular floor in a specified courtroom? When this happens, a disembodied voice announces over all the loudspeaker systems and speaker phones, "Attention all security personnel. This is a ten thirteen."

This announcement should be ignored by judges and lawyers. It is directed to the police, security officers, and a few selected secretaries who have been chosen as floor wardens. Among those who have managed to achieve that exalted office is my very own personal secretary. When the magic words "ten thirteen" are announced, she must run about and search for suspicious objects in the waste baskets on our side of the floor. Invariably, these announcements are made at the least convenient moments.

There was, for example, the time I had been hearing a complex construction dispute. For four days the attorneys questioned the contractor's accountant and scrutinized myriad invoices and subcontracts. Unknown to me, negotiations for settlement were being conducted in the public hall during the Court recesses, and at one point, the parties appeared so close to a settlement that they asked if I would see them in my office. I acceded to their request and returned to my office, followed by my usher and the attorneys.

We sipped a cup of coffee together and then began discussing the one remaining contentious point in their negotiations. After listening intently to each of them, I made a suggestion that I thought might be acceptable. There was a moment of silent reflection, followed by a loud announcement from my phone speaker, "Attention all security personnel. This is a ten thirteen."

My secretary burst through the office door saying, *"Alerte à la bombe! Alerte à la bombe!"*

She proceeded to peer into the waste basket on the floor beside my desk. Then she ran out saying, "I must verify all the waste baskets on the floor immediately."

The attorneys gasped, excused themselves, and left my office. That afternoon, they called to inform me that the case had been settled. Bombs do have a way of forcing decisions.

Somewhere along the line a sophisticated security system was installed in the public hall near the door to the judges' private quarters, to control the flow of visitors. Each judge's secretary has a small monitor that shows the hall and door between the public and private corridors. Traffic in this area is recorded constantly by concealed cameras, and the images are projected onto the screens of the monitor. When a visitor rings the bell to a judge's office, the camera's zoom lens focuses on the visitor's nose, so that each nostril is displayed on the screen larger than life. Each quivering hair of the visitor's beak (and sometimes moustache) sways in the wind of his breath.

The secretary has two buttons on the small box beneath the screen. One activates an intercom permitting her to communicate with the caller. The second button sounds a buzzer and releases the lock on the door to the private quarters. On quiet days, this system can provide hours of entertainment.

The moment the bell sounds, the secretary scrutinizes the upper lip and nostrils and inquires as to the identity of the caller. When he or she answers, she pushes the button to open the connecting door, all the while keeping her eye glued to the screen. The caller must run fifteen feet to open the door. As she sees him approach the door, she releases the buzzer button, presses on the intercom button, and barks, "Where are you?"

The caller returns to the intercom box only to hear the door buzzer sound again. Experienced secretaries can force a visitor to shuttle indefinitely between the door and the intercom. Knowledgeable lawyers always bring a student with them who stands ready to push the door open while the senior attorneys talk and display their noses to the inquisitive secretaries.

On days when a judge must receive many visitors, the secretaries simply thwart the security system by placing a thirty-five-pound free-standing ashtray where it will keep the door permanently ajar.

Judges are assigned their offices on the basis of seniority. So when a judge retires, a choice office on the upper floors becomes available and a junior judge is then offered the opportunity to ascend to the higher levels. At any moment in time, some judge, somewhere, is moving up in the palace.

The best suites are found on the south side of the sixteenth floor. The worst are above the cafeteria on the sixth floor, where one is exposed to the joint hazards of food odours and minor robberies from visitors to the criminal courts on the lower levels of the palace.

My original office was located on the seventh floor with a southern exposure. I would have enjoyed a splendid view of the St. Lawrence River had it not been for the black ventilation installations that rose ominously in front of my window like the walls of a prison.

Two years after my appointment, I was invited to move to the fifteenth floor. I use the expression "invited," because in certain circumstances such an invitation may be declined. Judges who have agreeable suite mates or particularly spacious offices may be reluctant to leave their original suites and will remain in more lowly premises. I, however, immediately accepted the offer to move my office to the north side of the fifteenth floor, since the new premises had an excellent view and were quieter and more prestigious than my original quarters.

The day after my move to the fifteenth floor, I was warmly greeted by a senior colleague, who informed me that the northern side of the fifteenth floor was undoubtedly the finest location in the courthouse. When the palace was constructed twenty years ago, he went on, he and several others had insisted on this location for their offices. In response to my puzzled look, he rattled off the benefits: northern exposure to counteract the shortcomings of the ventilation and air-conditioning system, proximity to the private elevators so that early departures could not be observed, and long distance from the office of the Chief Justice, who was inclined to assign difficult cases to the judges he saw most frequently.

I wondered if the colleague who had vacated my office for the loftier premises and panoramic views of the sixteenth floor was beginning to regret his move.

While judges are concerned with justice and liberty, others in the administration must deal with the more mundane task of making sure that the courthouse is properly maintained and that the facilities are kept in good repair. In our province, the role of administering public buildings is entrusted to "The Maintenance" and the Coordinator of Maintenance in the palace is Hubert Racine. Younger judges and palace officials refer to him as "Dr. No"; oldtimers call him "Rocket." The sobriquet is ironic, a relic from a previous era when the selfsame Rocket was reputed to be the fastest clerk in the criminal courts.

In his new responsibilities however, he has learned patience, obfuscation, and delay tactics. He has become a master of concealment, camouflage, and confusion, who cheerfully shuffles papers and requisitions, balances budgets, and manages his workforce in strict accordance with government policy and directives. In short, Rocket presides over the disintegration of the palace, achieves little, and satisfies few, all within the constraints of his budget.

A few days after moving to the fifteenth floor, my secretary informed me that Rocket had a special budget for repainting the offices of judges who relocate. I immediately instructed her to send him a written request to redecorate the suite and change the water-stained ceiling panels. The request was delivered during the first week of June. Two weeks later, Rocket sent me a memo acknowledging receipt, to which he attached a photocopy of my request so I would remember what I had requested.

The following month I received a further letter from Rocket, advising that my request was being processed but had not been approved. That September, I met Rocket in the elevator lobby. His face lit up as he confirmed that my request had been approved and he would invite bids as soon as the tender specifications were completed. I nodded and went off perplexed. Could the government possibly be calling for bids to paint one office with a small private bathroom? If so, why would they have to write a specification? All the judges' offices are identical in size. In fact, only two walls require painting because one wall is covered with bookcases and another consists entirely of windows.

In early October, two uniformed representatives of the Maintenance visited my office and spent an hour measuring the walls and drawing a diagram to scale. They showed me two hundred paint chips and invited me to choose a colour. Things were now moving along and I presumed that the tender call would be published shortly. Obviously, I had underestimated Rocket's attention to detail. Once weekly, throughout October, I received further visits from the representatives of the Maintenance, who remeasured my office to verify the accuracy of their plans and each time offered me the colour chips so I could select the colour of my choice — again.

In mid-November, Rocket appeared at the door of my suite to give me the good news that the contract had been signed. The following week the successful bidder paid a visit. He remeasured the two walls to satisfy himself that he had in fact bid on the correct specifications and invited me to select one of his colour chips. We had a pleasant conversation over coffee and he informed me that the office would be painted within the month.

Late one Wednesday afternoon, two weeks before Christmas, four appropriately clad painters appeared, pushing a small cart carrying two stepladders, paint, rags, and all the other implements of their trade. As I set off to a meeting, I observed that they were gracefully removing the curtains and throwing them in a pile on the floor. Upon my return two hours later, they were busily working away. One painter was working on each of the walls, a third was in the bathroom, and the fourth had managed to wiggle into the clothes closet, where he was happily brushing and rolling.

On Thursday morning, my office looked like a construction site, but the painters were nowhere to be seen. My patience was suitably rewarded, however, when they reappeared at four o'clock to apply the second coat of paint. The next morning, the job was complete. By that, I mean the walls had been repainted. The curtains were still piled in a heap on the floor, the doorknobs and light switches were covered with paper, and the furniture was askew. But these were mere trifles; the painting was done.

On Monday, I dropped by Rocket's office to express my appreciation. He wasn't in. In my exuberance, I had forgotten that Rocket doesn't work on Mondays. I went back the following day and there was Rocket, ready to receive me with warmth and grace. He glowed under my praise of his managerial skills and offered his services and those of the Maintenance whenever required, but subject to budgetary constraints. As I left his office, I could not resist the impulse to inquire how much the redecoration of my office had cost.

"*Monsieur le juge*," he replied, "$900 plus the usual administrative charges and of course my supervision, which is not invoiced."

"Rocket," I commented with a smile, "next time, allow me to bid on the job. I can get it done for $250: $25 for me, $25 for you, and $200 for the fellow who does the work."

My next project was to request an extra key to my new office. The one entrusted to me was not to be copied or reproduced without fear of punishment — as indicated by the command "reproduction prohibited" engraved on each key, which would deter all but the bravest or most larcenous of locksmiths.

After appropriate inquiry at the office of the Maintenance, I forwarded a written request for an additional key to the office of Rocket himself. Within a mere two weeks, he acknowledged receipt. However, despite seven further written requests, the matter has never been processed. Rocket's attention to detail is making me live in fear of the day when my one key will be misplaced.

The Maintenance is also in charge of the large directory boards in the dimly lit northern entrance hall, facing St. Antoine Street. This is a weighty responsibility, since the information desk is permanently abandoned, a victim of the last budget crisis in the Ministry of Justice. Visitors must rely completely on the information boards to locate the office of the judge they need to see.

When my office was moved from the seventh floor to the fifteenth, I paid little attention to the correction of the directory. After all, removing the plastic numerals after my name and substituting my new office numbers would not entail difficulty or expense. The numbers were not only available; they were already on the directory board opposite the name of the judge who had vacated my office. He, on the other hand, could be assigned the numbers of the previous occupant of his new office, who had moved elsewhere, and so on.

Six months after my move, I checked the directory. The changes had not been made, so I decided to get things moving. I instructed my secretary to write a letter to the Maintenance informing them that they had moved my furniture and painted my office, but somehow overlooked changing the directory on the ground floor.

"Why should they bother changing the directory?" she asked rhetorically, "the entrance is so dark you can't read the names without a flashlight. I hear that this is a new kind of security system to protect the judges. You can't harm what you can't find."

"Enough, enough," I replied. "Just send the letter. This one should be easy; it doesn't cost money."

That afternoon, I signed the letter and deposited it in the magic box for the internal messenger service. The system must have broken down because neither the letter nor its two subsequent reminders were even acknowledged.

That is how I came to drop by Rocket's office bright and early one Tuesday morning before he began his week's work.

"Merry Christmas, Hubert," I said. "This time I request a simple gift that will not have any impact on your budget."

"The Maintenance is always at your service, *Monsieur le juge*."

"Hubert, I am having trouble with mail and visitors because the directory board downstairs on the St. Antoine Street level has not been changed to indicate my new office number. Would you just lend me the key to the glass door and I shall go down and make the change personally."

"*Monsieur le juge*," he replied politely, "it is not so easy. Your name is not the only one with the wrong office number indicated. Half the board is wrong. There are so many changes happening around this building that we cannot keep up with the moves. Many of your colleagues have complained as well, but you must be patient. Everything will be solved in the next fiscal year."

"Hubert," I continued, "I know all about your fiscal year-end problems, but this is not a question of money. I insist that you make the changes and corrections this week. Otherwise, I warn you that I shall personally write and attach a note to the directory board which reads: 'Mr. Justice Steinberg removed his offices from the seventh floor to the fifteenth floor in July. Merry Christmas! This directory will be corrected by the Maintenance during the next fiscal year.' And I shall order that a guard be stationed beside the board to prevent the note from being removed. Do I make myself clear?"

"*Oui, Monsieur le juge*."

The following morning the directory board was corrected.

The final problem with my new office was the running toilet. From the day I moved to the fifteenth floor, the toilet kept flushing and making obscene noises. My repeated memos and phone calls to Rocket were acknowledged in writing, an army of plumbers made their way to my chambers, and repairs were performed and promised on each occasion, but the flow of unwanted water continued. The malfunctioning stopper or flapper valve did not prevent the toilet from being used, but the noise was a disturbance, and visitors were under the impression that I had concealed a lawyer or two in the washroom.

One warm June day, after labouring under this disadvantage for two years, I decided it was time to act. I instructed my secretary to locate Rocket. Alas, it was Monday; Rocket was unavailable. Fortunately, his assistant, Ms. Eve, responded. I explained my problem in detail to her. She listened sympathetically but informed me that problems of this nature were always handled by Rocket personally. Undaunted, I continued,

"Ms. Eve, undoubtedly you have heard the radio bulletins that Montreal is experiencing a water shortage this summer and residents are asked not to water their lawns. In the circumstances, how can I, as a Superior Court Judge, tolerate a toilet that has been running for two years. I shall not issue an injunction ordering you to fix my toilet on pain of fine and imprisonment, as some of my colleagues may be disposed to do. However, if the toilet is not fixed within one hour, I intend to convene a press conference and allow members of the *Fifth Estate* to personally witness this waste of precious water in provincial government buildings."

Two years and seven days after my first request, the flow of toilet waters stopped. Ms. Eve and I have become good friends and I am giving serious consideration to asking her for an additional key to my office.

The palace has a treasure room where the most prized and valuable possessions are stored safely. Its location is known to only a few of the oldest and most loyal employees. As far as I have been able to ascertain, none of the judges, not even the Chief, has been able to determine the whereabouts of this inner sanctum where Rocket preserves the courthouse valuables. Two secretaries, who have lived and worked in the palace for a total of fifty-five years, once whispered something of its contents to me: they had never seen them, but Rocket had given them a description once, in a moment of youthful indiscretion.

The treasure room is a repository for new furniture, skimmed-off orders, and antiques garnered from the offices of judges and ministers of justice who have long since departed. The contents of the sanctum are distributed sparingly among the privileged individuals whom Rocket wishes to reward. I am proud to have been the recipient of a fifteen-year-old scratched blond simulated oak coffee table, a coat rack of the same vintage, and the three mismatched chairs that embellish the reception area of my chambers. Others less fortunate than I must receive their guests on recycled bridge chairs.

Lest you think I exaggerate, I will share with you the stories of Judge A and Judge Z, who were both appointed to our court on the same day. Judge A was considered the senior of the two. His name appeared first on the order-in-council signed by the Governor General confirming the recommendation of Cabinet. Seniority entitled him to an office on the seventh floor. Regrettably, the previous occupant, whose name must remain secret, had promoted the office's three upholstered chairs to an upper floor. This was neither larcenous nor vindictive. His new office lacked chairs, because Rocket had sent eight chairs and one footstool from the upper floor out for re-upholstering. The last-minute decision had been made because the government's fiscal year had ended precipitously with $378.40 of the year's budget unspent. If it were not used up immediately, it would be lost to the department forever.

Justice A, filled with pride and enthusiasm after receiving the news of his appointment from the Minister of Justice, and basking in the warmth of the accolades of his partners, relatives, friends, new colleagues, and some old enemies, entered his office on the first morning and discovered that he would have to sit standing up. There was not a single chair in his new chambers. This would never do. He walked across the hall to consult one of his fellow judges and was referred to Rocket, whom he called immediately.

"Good morning, Mr. Racine. This is Mr. Justice A calling!"

"Good morning, *Monsieur le juge*. I congratulate you on your appointment. I trust that everything is in order. Remember, if you need anything at all, just call the Maintenance. We are here to serve you within the limits of the government's budget."

Judge A was encouraged by the reception. "As a matter of fact, there is one small deficiency in my office furniture. I do not have any chairs. Even now, I am speaking to you in a standing position."

"*Monsieur le juge*, I shall be there in ten minutes to investigate personally."

Within minutes Rocket appeared at the suite of Justice A. He introduced himself politely, looked around the room, checked the closet, and then returned to face the judge and said, "*Monsieur le juge*, you are absolutely right. There are no chairs in the office. I shall insist that the coordinator contact security services and demand an immediate investigation. I should appreciate it if you sent me a written request which I shall attach to my requisition. Naturally, you will receive copies of all relevant correspondence in this matter."

"But what about my chairs? I am a Superior Court Justice. I must receive people in my office, I must work here. When can I have three chairs?"

"*Monsieur le juge*, no stone will be left unturned in our investigation of this matter."

"I know, I know. But in the meantime, can you send me some chairs?"

"*Monsieur le juge*, the rules of the palace forbid me or anyone else from moving furniture from one room to another. You can well imagine what would happen to our inventory control system if people moved furniture about the palace freely. Besides, you are a judge and should not be obliged to use old furniture. Unfortunately, the government's fiscal year ends next month and the budget is exhausted, but I assure you that on April 1st, which is only five weeks from now, I shall prepare the documents and invite bids from several furniture manufacturers with whom we do business. I have no doubt you will have your new chairs before the summer, at the latest by Labour Day."

"But this is February. I must have a place to sit and work."

"*Monsieur le juge*, we at the Maintenance do our best within budgetary constraints. If you need anything else, please call me anytime, except Mondays. Good day." Rocket bowed slightly and left.

The Honourable Mr. Justice A was truly perplexed. In his old law firm he would have bellowed at his secretary and "temporarily" taken the chairs from the office of a junior associate. Ah, well, the Chief Justice had said to call if he had a problem.

Within three weeks, the Chief Justice had solved the problem. He had arranged for an investigation by his personal secretary, conferred with his associate Chief Justice, compelled the judge who had removed the chairs in the first place to promise to return them after receiving the re-upholstered chairs and arranged that this judge receive the first re-upholstered chairs to come back from the shop.

As for Mr. Justice Z, he was assigned quarters on the sixth floor. His new office was absolutely bare, though on his first visit he did locate a telephone perched atop the ventilation unit. Judge Z made the usual inquiries and was advised to call Hubert Racine, local representative of the Maintenance. The call began in the routine way.

"Good morning, Mr. Racine. This is Mr. Justice Z calling."

"Good morning, *Monsieur le juge*. I congratulate you on your appointment. Allow me to assure you that the Maintenance is here and available to help and serve you within the limits of our budget. Is there anything I can do for you?"

"Yes, as a matter of fact, there is one thing. I have no furniture whatsoever in my office."

"*Monsieur le juge*, I shall come to investigate, but as you know . . . ."

Suddenly, Mr. Justice Z recognized the voice at the other end of the line. It was a former clerk in the criminal courts whom he had known years ago. "Rocket, is that you?" he shouted.

"Yes, yes. Gerry, is that you?"

"You're damned right it's me. You better Rocket me an office full of furniture this afternoon or you won't sit for a week. Rocket down and see me now."

Within half an hour, the doors of the treasure room had opened. Four uniformed members of the Maintenance "found" bookcases, a desk, a credenza, three desk chairs, a sofa, a coffee table, an occasional chair, and a table, all of which were loaded onto dollies and delivered to the offices of Mr. Justice Z within the hour. Ten minutes later, Mr. Justice Z, seated and smiling behind his new desk, received a visit from his old friend Rocket, whom he embraced and greeted warmly.

I have compiled a list of simple questions which I propose to ask Rocket someday.

Why is access to the judges' elevator restricted by locked doors on all the floors except the second floor, which is the busiest in the building?

Why does the Maintenance install Kleenex paper holders in every private office and then refuse to provide Kleenex?

Why does the Maintenance refuse to provide holders for the toilet paper which they supply?

The most frequent requirement is communication with the courtroom. Ushers regularly run between the judge's office and the courtroom to deliver papers and advise if parties are ready. Why is the phone in the judge's private office able to communicate with every phone in the palace except the phones in the courtrooms?

What do the court clerks say to each other on the phones whenever the testimony gets interesting?

Why is there a continuing shortage of water glasses and a surfeit of water pitchers?

Why is it that every February the stationery store runs short of bench books for the judge to write notes in? I simply do not believe the excuse that this is because the government fiscal year-end occurs in March.

Why are the elevator doors in the private areas painted pink and blue on alternate floors?

III

On Stage

6

Conferences

Courts everywhere have been engulfed by the increasing volume and complexity of litigation — a situation that has spawned a plethora of proposals and techniques, both within and outside the justice system, to combat the situation. Private tribunals, mediation, and arbitration are a few of the alternatives to a formal hearing and judgment in civil cases. Within the system, attempts have been made to limit the duration of trials by requiring advance disclosure of evidence, out-of-court examinations, pre-trial conferences, and settlement conferences. Through a combination of intelligence, vigilance, the application of modern management techniques, and the introduction of organized pre-trial conferences, the Superior Court of Quebec has reduced the lengthy waiting periods between the initiation of court proceedings and the trial.

The annual schedule of assignments indicated that I would be assigned to pre-trial conferences for several months. I visited the Chief to determine whether this was a reward or a punishment. His reply was a model of Delphic ambiguity: "You have been chosen."

I rapidly learned that the purpose of these conferences is to meet the lawyers informally, review the file to make sure it is complete, encourage settlement discussions, define the issues in dispute, and when necessary fix a trial date convenient to the parties and their counsel.

Since I preside over pre-trial conferences only in cases that will be heard by other judges, I may express my opinion on the issues involved. The informal forum provides new, different, and often humorous insights.

At my very first conference, after greeting the attorneys and inviting them to sit down in the chairs opposite the desk, I peered at the plaintiff's counsel and commented, "I have studied this file and I find the plaintiff's case is particularly poor."

The plaintiff's attorney was taken aback. He wilted and was speechless. As the defendant's counsel sat upright, his chest expanded. I turned towards him and said, "And the defence is equally weak."

I continued, "In the circumstances, this case is a prime candidate for settlement. Rather than fix a trial date and risk embarrassment to both of you, I suggest that you discuss this matter here and now. I shall withdraw for a few minutes."

The dazed attorneys requested that the conference be put over to the following week to permit them to meet privately. I complied with their request. Three days later, I received a letter informing me that the case had been settled. I had earned my spurs.

To facilitate the preparation of dockets and court rolls, standard time periods are used instead of calendar months. These periods are similar to, but do not coincide with, the calendar months. Each period begins on a Monday, ends on a Friday, and contains either four or five weeks. As a result, it is not unusual for our April term to begin on Monday, April

2nd, and to end on Friday, May 4th. The spillover into the subsequent month is even greater when the period is five weeks.

One year I had been presiding at pre-trial conferences for the April term. The file was incomplete and I asked the attorneys to examine a witness in the presence of a court stenographer before the term expired.

"Mr. Lavoie," I said, "my assignment in this division ends this month, so I must insist that you complete the examination and return for a further conference before the end of the April term. Will May 3rd be convenient?"

Lavoie looked at me as though I had taken leave of my senses. I realized the incongruity of my remarks and explained, "Mr. Lavoie, as you know, Pope Gregory established a calendar that is followed throughout the Western world. Allow me to inform you that it is not the only calendar in existence. Chief Justice Gold has also established a calendar, and in the calendar of my Chief Justice, the month of April ends on May 4th this year. Is that clear?"

Lavoie nodded his head in feigned comprehension and dutifully noted the date on his agenda. At the conclusion of the conference, I saw the attorneys to the door. As they walked down the corridor, I overheard Lavoie remark to his adversary, "Wait till I tell my partners the judges are now quoting St. Grégoire!"

Receiving groups of attorneys at the rate of three a day generated an air of activity not usually found in judges' offices in the palace. But in the midst of this holus-bolus, I discovered that the smallest courtesy could yield impressive results. Even a cup of coffee offered to attorneys as they entered my office helped contribute to a more relaxed atmosphere. This routine did cause some problems, however.

Towards the end of the second week, my secretary disappeared for half an hour at a rather inconvenient time. When

I asked where she'd been, she replied that she had been out buying coffee.

"Didn't you disappear for an hour last week with the same excuse?"

"Of course," she replied, "what do you expect, the way you drag every Tom, Dick, and Harry out of the corridors and offer them coffee. And while we're on the subject, why don't you get some paper cups like Judge Mass? *His* secretary doesn't have to spend her day washing coffee mugs."

I could handle difficult lawyers, but obviously did not impress my own secretary.

As she sat down at her desk, I glanced over her shoulder. She was typing a letter inviting Mrs. Betty MacCormack to a pre-trial conference.

"What is that file all about?" I asked.

"Some woman is acting on her own behalf," she replied. "Apparently she had a lawyer, but he withdrew from the file after the date was fixed for the pre-trial conference. So I am writing to her home to confirm the details."

"In French?"

"Yes. I don't know whether she speaks French or English."

"You might have guessed she speaks English from her name, Betty MacCormack."

"Well, I didn't. Besides, her husband's name is Mikael. I don't know many English people called Mikael. In fact, I don't know any."

"Well," I responded, "I know at least one Mikael MacCormack and you should too. His name was all over the newspapers last summer. Some kind of political scandal. I don't remember the details. I'll bet it's the same fellow. Write his wife a letter in English."

"I don't have an English form," she shot back.

"I shall be happy to make one up for you."

"It won't be necessary because I have already typed the

letter in French. If she doesn't understand, she can call the office and ask for an English letter."

"You are prejudiced against women. I'll bet you would write in English if you were writing to Mr. MacCormack."

"I would not. Not unless he called me."

"Well, how do you expect Mrs. MacCormack to call you if she doesn't understand the letter. Put an English P.S. at the bottom inviting her to call you if she doesn't understand the letter."

"Okay, but only if you take back the insult. You called me prejudiced."

"I take it back. Add the P.S."

"Okay, it's a deal."

I was not surprised the following week when Jackie sheepishly informed me that she had received a call from Mrs. Betty MacCormack requesting an English version of the letter. She had prepared a draft translation but needed my help to polish some of the phrases.

"When you finish sending the letter, please leave the file in my office so I can see what it's all about," I said.

"She sounds like a real lady," my secretary volunteered. "We have to do something for her."

"I see that we are over our anti-women prejudices. We will look at the file in our office with our door closed."

The application for divorce was routine. It mentioned the fact that the couple had been married in Egypt. Mikael had been born in Eastern Europe of British parents and Betty was Canadian by birth. They had two children now at university who were supported by their father. Betty sought a lump-sum payment of one million dollars as well as the ownership of the family residence and a Mercedes automobile. These were substantial demands, but perhaps they were justified.

As I leafed through the more recent documents, I noticed that Betty's attorney had withdrawn from the file and had not been replaced. The last document in the file was a one-year-old copy of *Time* magazine with a picture of Mikael on the cover. I had no idea how the magazine came to be in the Court file, but I could not resist the temptation to read the cover story. After all, this was hardly confidential information.

According to the article, Mikael was a successful arms dealer who had made a fortune during the war between Iran and Iraq by selling arms to both sides. He was a friend of politicians and a prominent supporter of both major political parties. He enjoyed fast cars and was frequently seen in the company of beautiful women. He had apartments in New York, London, Zurich, and Cairo. His villa in Cannes was equipped with a swimming pool in the shape of an M. In his spare time, he had designed a line of men's sportswear which bore an insignia in the shape of an M. The article mentioned his pending divorce but made no other mention of his wife. Well, since she was representing herself, I would have a chance to meet her at the pre-trial conference. Undoubtedly, Mikael would be represented by his attorney, Robert Calvin.

On the day of the conference Betty MacCormack arrived early. My secretary received her while I remained in my office. She called to brief me.

"She looks nice. Please try to help her. I will phone you when Calvin arrives."

"Good," I responded, "and make sure you treat him equally well. Offer him a coffee in those new plastic cups."

At precisely three o'clock, the Court clerk entered my office followed by Betty MacCormack and Robert Calvin. We shook hands; I invited them to be seated and began the meeting.

"I see that both parties seek a divorce. Mrs. MacCormack seeks a lump-sum payment of $1 million, as well as the home and automobile. Which of those demands are contested?"

Robert Calvin replied, "There is no contestation respecting the family home. It is registered in the name of Mrs.

MacCormack, and my client makes no claim for the home. As to the car, he is prepared to sign it over to his wife, provided that he is not thereby obligated for the repairs and for a replacement when the car is no longer useable. The main issue in dispute is the claim for $1 million, which my client cannot afford. Since the end of the war between Iran and Iraq war, his income has been considerably reduced."

"Mrs. MacCormack," I said, "I would like to hear what you have to say. But first, please tell me why you are no longer represented by an attorney. This is a substantial claim. Your attorney has withdrawn from the record. I am fearful that you will not be able to present this claim in the best light and deal with any technical issues that may arise. The practice of law is a complicated matter and requires formal training."

"Sir," she replied, "I was represented by one of the larger offices in the city. I simply cannot afford to pay their fees. I am not poor enough to qualify for legal aid, and I don't have the money to pay for expensive lawyers. Besides, it won't make any difference."

"I think it will make a difference. Do you want me to postpone the conference so that you can engage a lawyer, or even help you find one?"

"No sir," she answered. "May I tell you my story?"

"The purpose of the conference is to shorten the duration of the trial, to arrange a settlement if possible, and to fix a trial date," I said.

"If you would allow me to tell my story, I think you could understand why I am here, and then arrange a date and whatever else is required."

"I am listening."

"Mikael and I were married twenty years ago. I was young at the time and impressed by his foreign, almost exotic ways. He was older than me. For the first few years, it was very exciting. We went out, travelled a great deal, and he introduced me to many important people. It was great! Like in the movies. When our first son was born, things changed. Mikael seemed to stay away and travel more often. I was left alone with our son. Things got even worse after our second son was born. It's true that I had a beautiful house, a fancy car, and a maid, but I seemed to be alone all the time. I thought that things would improve after the boys started going to school."

"Did they?"

"No. I guess it was too late. Between his business, his political friends and, I guess, his girlfriends, things just got worse and worse between us. Oh, I would fall in love with him again whenever he would stay home for a while. It was so exciting to be together. But then I think he would just get bored with me and the boys, and he would leave after a few days."

"You will be able to explain all of this to the trial judge. I have to ask you to only tell me recent events which will indicate the possible length of the trial and lead to settlement or shortening of the trial."

"Please, I am almost finished. Well, after a while I arranged my own social life and became occupied with different charities and social clubs. I know that Mikael approved. Even though we were apart more, we got on better when we were together. Well, one day I picked up this copy of *Time* at the corner store. Mikael's picture was on the cover. I took the magazine home and that night I read the story."

"Are you referring to the magazine that was filed into the court record?"

"Yes, I sent that magazine to court last month when I realized it had not been filed by my lawyer."

"It is not admissible," interjected Robert Calvin. "It's not the best evidence."

"The trial judge will decide that," I replied. "Please finish, Mrs. MacCormack."

"Well," she continued, "you may not believe this, but I

found out by reading the magazine article that I was about to be divorced. I guess I should have known it would happen but I didn't. I always hoped that some day we would work things out. You can fool yourself, but only up to a point. When you read in a magazine that your husband wants a divorce, you cannot pretend any longer."

"So what happened?"

"The story becomes even more bizarre. I called Mikael in France and asked him if it was true and why he didn't have the decency to at least tell me before informing the world. Wait till you hear this. He told me that the divorce wasn't serious, that he still loved me, and that he was doing it for tax reasons. Well, I may be naïve, but there is a limit. Even I wouldn't accept that explanation."

"I can understand."

"He said that his lawyer would call upon me and make a generous offer of settlement."

"Did Mr. Calvin contact you?"

"No, sir, he was not my husband's lawyer at the time."

"That's correct," Calvin interjected. "I only took over this file after the legal proceedings were issued."

"My husband was represented by Ron Martin, the member of Parliament. He came to my house the next day, told me the same lie, that my husband was prepared to pay me $1 million and let me keep the house and the car, and would give me any other help needed to adjust. He showed me a contract signed by my husband and he asked me to sign."

"Did you?"

"Yes. I know Mikael. He is too rich and too strong for me to fight. He always gets his own way. I knew that I had no choice, so I signed."

"You did not even try to contact a lawyer?"

"No, it would not have helped. I signed and I trusted Mikael to keep his word."

"Do you have the contract?"

"Yes, here it is, sir. It is only two small pages. You can look and see that it says he will pay me $1 million."

Turning to Calvin, I asked, "Is the contract admitted? Is all this true?"

"Yes, my lord," he replied. "Everything Mrs. MacCormack has said is true, except that her husband is not rich. He has lost all his properties and cannot afford to pay the $1 million. His income has evaporated."

"What about his cars?" asked Mrs. MacCormack. "He always boasted they were worth a fortune."

"They were not his cars, even though he had the use of them," answered Calvin. "They belonged to a company that manufactured clothing with the M insignia. He used the cars to advertise the sports clothes. The company is now bankrupt and the cars have been repossessed."

"All of them?" I asked.

"Yes," replied Calvin. "All except a four-door Buick which Mikael drives when he is in Montreal. You know the car, Mrs. MacCormack. He used to keep it as a spare auto for use when the others were in the garage. He has no other cars now."

"Mr. Calvin, has your client provided sworn statements attesting to all of this?"

"No, my Lord, but he is willing to do so."

"Fine," I said. "In that case, he will not object to my order that he file into the court record, within the next thirty days, copies of his income tax returns for the past five years, photographs of all real estate owned by him, together with a copy of the latest real estate tax bills, latest insurance policies insuring these homes and their contents, the same respecting any cars he may own and the latest financial statements of every company in which he holds more than 5 percent of the issued shares or has a right to acquire such interest."

"There is no objection," responded Calvin, "but my client is no longer a Canadian resident and doesn't file income tax returns. As to the rest, I shall fax him today."

"How long will the trial last?" I inquired.

"No more than one day. My client does not own any significant assets and as you can see, most of the facts will be admitted."

"Mrs. MacCormack. Once again, do you want to engage a lawyer? He will be more adept than you at questioning your husband in court."

"No, sir, I don't think it will help. I will represent myself and I hope the judge will understand the case as you do."

"I can assure you that I shall not be the presiding judge. I conduct these conferences in cases that will be heard by other judges. In that way, I can express my opinion without hesitation. My comments remain confidential."

Turning to Calvin, I continued, "Mr. Calvin, I will not even express a confidential opinion respecting this case. I invite you to deduce what I think."

I turned back to Mrs. MacCormack, "Mrs. MacCormack, when do you want the trial to be held?"

"The last week of February," she answered.

"My lord, my client will be in Zermatt at that time."

"Wrong, Mr. Calvin. He will be in Court for his divorce hearing on February 26th, at nine-thirty in the morning. Does that date suit you?"

"Yes, my lord."

"The conference is now ended. If my order to produce documents is not respected, I shall be available to make further orders to assure compliance."

"That won't be necessary," said Calvin. "Your order will be strictly observed."

"Thank you. One final word, Mrs. MacCormack. Please hire a lawyer."

"Thank you, sir. I promise to think about it. Thank you, sir." Betty MacCormack rose and left my office, followed by Robert Calvin.

"*Bien*," said my secretary as she entered my office. "Did

you help her? What else can we do for her? She is a real lady. Just like I said."

"Yes, she is a lady. I did what I could. I guess all you can do now is pray. I sure hope she hires a lawyer."

I put the matter out of my mind and turned to other things. In fact, I had forgotten all about the case until the afternoon of February 26th. When I returned from court to my office that day, my secretary was waiting.

"She was here, and she left you a note. The note is on your desk."

"Who was here?"

"Betty MacCormack. Have you forgotten about her so soon?"

I walked into my office without comment. It had been a difficult day, but my tiredness disappeared when I read the handwritten note.

Your Lordship —

I represented myself and I won! Thank you so much!

Betty M.

At some conferences the mundane task of selecting a date and estimating the length of the trial becomes a particular challenge. This was always the case when the defendant was represented by Robert Bochatz, undoubtedly one of the most difficult attorneys to control.

A fellow judge had clipped a note to the court file.

Please see if you can do something with this character. He failed to show up for two meetings in my office. I hesitate to cite him for contempt because he has already been disbarred for three months for misconduct during a trial before me.

On looking through the file, I saw that the plaintiff had sued for damages after discovering that the electrical wiring in the home purchased from Bochatz's client was inadequate, the drainage system was blocked, and the roof leaked. The defendant claimed these defects were disclosed before the offer to purchase was made. This case would require two days for trial.

As I waited patiently for Bochatz, I speculated as to how I would react if he failed to attend. After all, he had stood up my colleague on two occasions without even a phone call or apology. My musings were cut short, though, for he surprised me by appearing punctually.

After the initial introductions and formalities, I began to discuss the case with the attorneys.

"Gentlemen, I see this is a claim for damages resulting from the sale of a private residence . . . "

"And fraud," interjected Bochatz.

"I didn't see any mention of fraud in the written proceedings," I responded.

"It's implied, if not specifically alleged," said Bochatz.

At this point I turned to Norman Brown, who represented the plaintiff, "Mr. Brown, is it your intention to prove fraud?"

"No, my lord, it is not alleged and will not be proven."

"Don't believe him," interrupted Bochatz. "He will try to prove fraud and my client is entitled to make a full and complete defence. That is why I believe the trial will last two weeks. I have at least seventeen witnesses . . . "

"Mr. Bochatz," I interrupted, "you have heard the statement that there are no allegations of fraud and the plaintiff will not try to establish fraud."

"My lord, this is an infringement of the Charter of Rights. Every citizen is entitled to defend his interests fully before the courts."

"Mr. Bochatz," I sighed, "the right to defend oneself is limited to those cases where one is attacked."

I turned to Norman Brown. "Mr. Brown, are you authorized to confirm to me in writing on behalf of the plaintiff that no evidence of fraud will be presented at trial?"

"Yes, my lord," he said. "It was never our position that a fraud has been committed. The issues are simple. The roof, plumbing, and wiring require extensive repair. We have no objection to the defendant's experts examining the building. The only question is whether or not these defects were disclosed before the offer was signed."

Mr. Bochatz spoke up. "They never offered me the chance to send experts to examine the building. That places a new problem before us. It will take me at least four months to hire experts and get a report."

"Bochatz," I said impatiently, "I have some experience in this area. I know you can get experts to examine the house in one week. People do it all the time when they offer to purchase properties. Do you want to have the house examined by an expert?"

"I don't know. I must speak to my client."

"Mr. Bochatz, here is the phone. Do it now."

"Oh, no, my client is in Florida. It would be long distance."

"Mr. Bochatz, place the call. The government will happily pay the long distance charges."

"I don't know his telephone number."

"Call your office and get it."

"My secretary isn't working today."

"Mr. Bochatz, I have the impression that you are stalling. I shall give you two weeks to examine the property and get an expert's report if you so wish. The report must be filed in the court record within three weeks, and I shall fix the trial for two days."

"My lord, two days would not be sufficient. I have told you that I require two weeks to present my witnesses to defend the fraud charges."

"There is no fraud charge. Your opponent has undertaken

to file a written admission to that effect and I shall obtain it before you leave my office today."

"I don't believe him."

"Bochatz, I shall fix the trial for two days with the proviso that if there is any proof of fraud, your client will be entitled to make a complete defence. Is that understood?"

"Yes."

"Today is October 7th. You may have two weeks to obtain and file an expert's report. That should take until the end of October. I can fix the trial date for January 23rd. Is that convenient?"

"No," replied Bochatz, "I told you that my client is now in Florida. He lives in Montreal and spends the winter in Florida. As you know, it is difficult to travel back and forth between different climates."

"Mr. Bochatz, is your client a sick man?"

"No."

"Bochatz, how old is your client?"

"Forty-six."

At this point, Norman Brown stood up and pointed at Bochatz and said, "My lord, this is the third conference. Mr. Bochatz did not show up for the first two before your colleague."

"I know."

"I met Mr. Bochatz today for the first time and I cannot endure him. I have been practising law for twelve years and I know that I will not survive a trial of one week or even two days with that man. I request your permission to withdraw from this file. My client will have to find a younger and more patient attorney."

"Mr. Brown, I will adjourn this conference so that you can speak to your client. If he agrees with your withdrawal from the file, I have no objection."

Brown rose, shook hands with me, glared at Bochatz, and left the office. Bochatz looked up at me with his most innocent look and commented: "I wonder what made him so mad."

"It must be the weather," I observed. "As winter approaches, both the days and people's tempers become shorter."

N.P. was short of breath a she rushed in my office carrying two briefcases. Her clothing was slightly awry and her blonde hair dishevelled. "I'm sorry I'm late," she panted. "I was tied up in another courtroom. I represent the lion lady."

I motioned her to an empty chair, glanced at the two other attorneys who had been waiting in my office for the last fifteen minutes, and instructed the court clerk to record the names of the attorneys and their clients so that the pre-trial conference could begin. N.P.'s client had a strangely lyrical and alliterative name. The other lawyers represented the insurers of a pharmaceutical company and a veterinarian.

Before I could say more, N.P. began, "I love the circus. I have learned all about the circus while preparing this case. It's a wonderful place. The people are so interesting. I spent two years working on this file."

"Tell me about the lion lady," I said. "All I know about this file is that your client is claiming $1 million from a pharmaceutical company and a veterinarian. What is this all about?"

The attorney for the vet began to say something, but N.P. beat him to the draw.

"My client is a professional lion trainer. For six years she devoted herself to finding and training lions for a travelling circus." She caught her breath, straightened up in her chair, and continued, "Two years ago, the circus arrived in Sherbrooke for a two-week stay. When the circus paraded into town, my client had noticed a veterinarian's office in the town square.

"That afternoon, several of the lions seemed out of sorts. This has happened before and is a kind of travel sickness. One particular drug is available on the market and cures this sickness immediately. No prescription is necessary. So she went to the vet's office, bought the capsules, and gave them to the lions. The next morning, when she went to see her lions, they were all dead. Can you imagine how terrible that was? Those lions were her children, her livelihood, her companions."

"Perhaps you can tell me more about the medicine?" I asked.

"It was clearly marked, 'for horses only'!" interjected the attorney for the pharmaceutical manufacturer.

"That doesn't matter," continued N.P. as she reached into one of her briefcases. "I have jurisprudence that says that if the manufacturer knows his product is being used for other purposes he must take special precautions, and they knew these capsules were being administered to other animals."

"Not lions," he responded.

"Besides, they changed the prescription and didn't modify the packaging. The colours and format of the new formula were the same."

"The change made it more effective and didn't present any additional side effects on horses."

"What about lions?"

"We don't manufacture drugs for lions!"

"You should have known the change could be lethal for lions."

Their voices started to rise. I turned to the attorney for the vet and asked, "What is your client's position?"

"My client specializes in horses," he answered. "His office is in the midst of several farming communities and he only treats horses. He never examined a lion in his life and did not give any professional opinion. This woman with the funny name came to his office and ordered the capsules by trade name. She gave him $17.50 for them and left. How could he be expected to know she would feed them to lions and they would die?"

"You don't seem to realize that my client lost her lions and was deprived of her livelihood," N.P. interjected.

"And my client has suffered as well. Ever since this action was taken, he has had nightmares about lions and has decided to retire. His insurance is less than the $1 million claimed and he is not a rich man."

A change of topic was necessary to defuse the passions.

"I guess it will not be possible to agree on responsibility," I said, "so perhaps we can advance matters by discussing the amount of damages. One million dollars is a lot of money. How do you arrive at that figure? What were your client's previous earnings? How much does a lion cost?"

"Six hundred dollars per lion," commented the attorney for the drug company. "We will pay her $3,000 for her lions, throw in another $5,000 for training and loss of income . . . say $10,000 . . . plus costs, and let's settle."

"No, no," replied N.P. "I know that a lion costs only $600, but the cost of the lion is nothing. My client trained those animals for years. It took her six years to train those lions."

"How can you say that? We have proof that she bought three of the lions only two years before the accident."

"Those three," said N.P. with disdain, "you cannot put your head in their mouth. They weren't completely trained. They were only cubs. They were there for decoration. They were not the real performers. The others, it took years to train them."

"Leave the lions aside for a moment," I said. "What was your client's income in the previous and subsequent years?"

N.P.'s eyes sparkled. "You understand, she claims more than the value of the lions. This is like a bodily injury case where the victim is unable to work. She could not work after her act died."

"Her tax returns show an income of $8,000 to $10,000 for

each of the previous three years," commented the lawyer for the vet.

"I know," she answered, "but the trend was upward. My client spent five years of her life developing this act and she was just about to break into the big time. This was the year when she could begin to make $50,000 to $60,000. The training of the lions was completed and she was becoming known as a special attraction. Her income was going up each week."

"What happened to her income after the accident?" I asked. "There is a duty to mitigate or minimize the damages."

"Her income rose to $20,000 the following year," said the counsel for the drug manufacturers. "Here is a copy of her tax returns."

"Oh, that was a lucky break," responded N.P. "She was able to get a tiger act going."

"Wait a minute," I said. "I do not know much more about animal training than I have learned this afternoon. Do tigers take as long to train as lions? More time? Less time?"

"About the same," replied N.P. with authority.

"Then explain how she was able to perform with tigers the following month," interjected the attorney for the veterinarian.

"Easy," said N.P. "I said she had a lucky break. She bought an act from the elephant lady."

"I'm sorry, but you've lost me again," I said. "Did you say she bought tigers from the elephant lady?"

"Yes," said N.P., losing patience. "In the circus, elephants don't require all that much attention. So the elephant lady trained tigers in her spare time. She was called the elephant lady, but she could just as well have been called the tiger lady, because she had a tiger act."

"Well, if the elephant lady had a tiger act, and if it takes years to train tigers, why would the elephant lady sell her tigers?"

"Because she had an accident."

"I trust she wasn't bitten by a tiger."

"No, she was squashed by an elephant and had to retire."

"I think I'm beginning to understand . . ." I said.

It was apparent that the parties would never agree on the amount of damages and a settlement would not be found that day. After further discussion, I fixed a trial date in the fall.

"I think I shall ask the Chief Justice to auction off the privilege of hearing this case," I commented.

"Oh," N.P. enthused. "Please hear this case yourself. You understand animals and the circus so well."

"Thank you," I said, smiling, "but my docket's full already. I don't have time to wander down the Yellow Brick Road."

7

On and Off
the Bench

Each day hundreds of people receive a subpoena or order compelling them to drop everything and come to court to file documents, describe events, and participate in the resolution of a dispute. The subpoenas are prepared in the office of an attorney or by a clerk of the court.

Competent attorneys contact and interview witnesses in advance and try to organize trials as to cause them the least possible inconvenience. Regrettably, some attorneys scatter subpoenas like buckshot, oblivious to the consequences and disruptions to the lives of the people who are served. All too frequently, uninformed witnesses are compelled to wait for endless periods in the corridors of the courthouse, unaware of why they have been summoned, what is being disputed, or when they will testify. It is up to the judge to make sure that they are treated with as much courtesy and consideration as possible.

My usher always investigates the public corridors at the

beginning of a trial. If she informs me that there are more than two or three people clustered around the entrance to the courtroom, I ask the attorneys if it would be possible to minimize the inconvenience to witnesses who are not personally interested in the suit and have been summoned to file a document or report on one or more facts that are not seriously contended. The attorneys will frequently agree that some witnesses can be released after filing a document and that the attendance of others may be replaced by a simple admission by one of the parties.

In the hearing itself, witnesses are not usually represented by attorneys and the judge must ensure that they be treated fairly and courteously — particularly in the case of inexperienced witnesses caught in the crossfire of rising tempers in a hotly contested lawsuit.

"Justice must not only be done but must manifestly be seen to be done" is the classic formulation of the judge's duty to ensure that the trial is conducted fairly and in a calm, dispassionate atmosphere. People in the courtroom often derive their impression of the legal system from the process as well as from the result. An irascible judge or a rude and aggressive attorney may create tensions that distort the testimony and ultimate outcome of a suit; humour can be misunderstood and should often be restrained. Throughout, a balance must be found which meets the expectations of the parties, witnesses, and observers, maintains the respect and dignity of the system, and is faithful to the principles of law.

The court clerk asks each witness his name, address, and age. Amazingly, many are surprised and even embarrassed by the latter question. But some are prepared for it, as one of my colleagues discovered during a sitting in New Carlisle. The witness was a very proper lady wearing a hat and white gloves. After taking the oath she was asked her age.

"Forty years and a few months," she replied.

The judge peered over his glasses and inquired, "How many months is a few?"

"Two hundred and forty-three if you must know," the witness responded.

Witnesses require air space and are entitled to the courtesy of having the lawyers who question them remain at a distance. Unfortunately, certain members of the Bar tend to move closer and closer as the interrogation proceeds. After ten minutes, these attorneys end up less than two feet from the witness, whom they assault with bad breath, a spray of saliva, and occasional body odours. The witness is intimidated and will say anything to end the discomfort. I am constantly alert to this situation and frequently interject to remind attorneys to keep their distance. If my reminder is ignored and the practice continues, my usher places a glass of water between the lawyer and the witness and we both wait and hope that the witness will spill the water on the attorney's papers or clothes. The results are most effective.

Remarkably, the attorneys who have suffered this indignity never seem to learn or change, and they resort to the same offensive habits at the next session. So my water pitcher is constantly full and ready.

Justice Pierre Pinard tells of a case where the defence attorney was a heavy cigar smoker whose breath could cause discomfort. While questioning the chief witness for the prosecution, he moved closer and closer, holding his pencil like an imaginary cigar. As the stale fumes and heavy breath continued their assault, the witness looked him in the eye and said, "Step back. You stink!" The judge and the jury were unable to contain their laughter, and a short adjournment was called.

The quick-witted attorney was equal to the challenge. During the adjournment his associate ran across the street and purchased an atomizer for him. When the trial resumed the attorney sprayed his throat with an elaborate and exaggerated gesture in the presence of the witness and jury before asking the question once again.

Despite the many court dramas on TV, witnesses still seem surprised by the extent of the questioning they must undergo. In one trial an elderly gentleman who was being examined in great detail as to the value of his assets looked up at me in despair and asked, "Do I have to answer all these questions? Why does the lawyer ask questions when he knows the answers?"

"Sir," I replied, "in this courtroom everyone has a job to perform. The lawyer's job is to ask questions, yours is to answer them, and my job is to listen."

He nodded his head and the trial continued.

The regular use of French and English in the Montreal courts can give rise to unexpected situations. Court clerks often deduce the language of the witness by their name and manner, and sometimes they err.

As one witness approached, the clerk instructed her, "*Madame, mettez votre main droite sur la Bible.*"

When she failed to acknowledge the instruction, the clerk repeated, "*Madame, mettez votre main droite sur la Bible.*"

The witness looked ahead, uncomprehending. The clerk now realized the situation and inquired, "Madam, are you English?"

"No, I am Polish," she responded.

"Do you speak English?"

"Yes."

The clerk continued, "Place your right hand on the Bible. Do you promise to tell the truth, the whole truth, and nothing but the truth?"

"Yes, I will."

At this point, the plaintiff's attorney addressed me in halting English.

"*Monsieur le juge*, I practise in a small town forty miles from Montreal and do not speak the language of Shakespeare."

"*Maitre*," I replied with a grin, "do you speak the language of Chopin?"

"*Non, Monsieur le juge.*"

"In that case," I continued, "you will have to proceed in English as well as you can and I shall be pleased to assist you."

Problems of comprehension can also arise when the witness is not completely fluent in the language of the trial. Sometimes the witness is simply puzzled, though, and rephrasing the question resolves the problem. In one such case, the witness was a seventy-year-old woman of Austrian descent. Her grasp of English was imperfect. The counsel began:

"Madam, you are a defendant in this case?"

"I wouldn't know," she answered.

I leaned forward and asked her: "Are you being sued?"

"Of course," she responded with a triumphant smile.

At other times, the witness may reply to the question understood rather than the one asked.

Justice Tannenbaum recounts the story of a witness who was asked the introductory question, "Do you know the plaintiff?"

The witness responded in a heavy accent, "He's not a plain thief, he's a dirty rotten thief."

Justice Morris Fish of the Quebec Court of Appeal delights in telling the story of the witness in criminal proceedings who was about to give testimony that would incriminate him. Under the then prevailing law, a judge in such cases could grant the witness the protection of the court, and thereafter the testimony given could not be presented against the witness in subsequent criminal proceedings.

The Judge: My good man, I offer you the protection of the Court.

The Witness: Thank you, Your Honour, but it is not necessary. I receive regular social welfare payments.

In the course of their careers, many judges develop a keen, though dry, sense of humour and an acerbic tongue. While patient and courteous listening are the hallmarks of the judge, these other "weapons" may be necessary to maintain order, to control an overly talkative witness, to limit redundant argument, or to ease tensions.

Justice Mackay is known for his stern demeanour and strict control of his courtroom. Once, as he was about to pronounce judgment, an attorney sitting in the audience and wearing a gown rose to address him. Justice Mackay glared at the intruder to no avail. He then asked, "Who, may I ask, are you?"

"An *amicus curiae*," the attorney responded.

"In this room," uttered Justice Mackay, "I am the *curia*, and you, sir, are no friend of mine."

The intruder sat down and remained silent.

Justice Fraser Martin was assigned a large courtroom usually used by a three-man commission. He entered and sat in the centre chair behind the extended desk. The attorney for the plaintiff requested a twenty-minute adjournment because his first witness had been delayed. Justice Martin looked solemnly at the vacant chair on his right, then at the chair on his left and responded, "My colleagues and I are all of the opinion that your request should be granted."

In a case where I presided, one young lawyer continued to repeat each question so many times that he single-handedly transformed a two-day trial into a five-day saga. Throughout, I listened patiently, while trying to find a way to wind things up.

On the Friday morning, his senior partner entered the courtroom and quietly sat down at the counsel desk. Perhaps he had come to see what had happened to his young associate.

By now my patience was exhausted. As I heard the same question repeated for the fifth time, I pushed my chair back noisily and stared at the clock. The flustered attorney looked at me and said, "I am not trying to bore the Court."

"Young man," I replied caustically, "at times in life, one succeeds without trying!"

The senior partner rose and left without comment. The trial ended two hours later.

When he was in Superior Court, Justice Amédée Monet encountered a similar problem while hearing a divorce application. Although sufficient evidence was presented to justify the granting of a divorce on the grounds of adultery, the attorney asked his client to describe her husband's actions under the guise of establishing mental cruelty as well. Since he had already decided that the grounds were sufficient, Justice Monet was reluctant to hear this additional unnecessary evidence. He leaned forward and said to the attorney, "How *many* divorces are you seeking today?"

One litigant discovered his own solution to the problem of the overly talkative witness. His wife droned on and on, describing each matrimonial dispute in great detail. When I glanced at the husband, he was fast asleep. Perhaps his inattention was the real grounds for divorce.

A problem may arise where an attorney or party is personally known to the judge. Obviously, if a relative is involved, the matter must be referred to another judge for hearing, but some situations are less clear.

Saundrah was a young, attractive professional, whose marriage had been brief and childless. I had met members of both her family and her husband's family socially on several occasions and heard of their reputed wealth. Her application for increase in alimony so she could buy a sports car was delivered to my office. In the circumstances, I suggested that the matter be tried by another judge. A month later, I encountered Saundrah's attorney in the corridor of the palace, who told me, "Saundrah is very upset. She doesn't understand why you wouldn't hear her application for an increase in alimony."

"I didn't know you were aware I had declined the file," I responded, "but in any event, you can tell Saundrah I would not have given her a nickel because I know her father owns a substantial share of the city of Winnipeg and gave her an apartment building on her twenty-first birthday."

"Thank you," replied her lawyer, "I'm glad you didn't hear us, and Saundrah is no longer insulted."

One day I entered the courtroom to hear an argument in law and found myself facing R.T., my next-door neighbour. I immediately mentioned that I was reluctant to hear the arguments and suggested the matter be sent to another courtroom.

"My Lord," R.T. responded, "I have informed my opponents of the fact that we are neighbours. They and I consent to your hearing this application and ask the court clerk to note our consent in the record."

His opponents stood and reiterated their agreement. In the circumstances, I invited the attorneys to proceed. Two hours later, I dismissed R.T.'s application.

The next morning, when I opened the front door to retrieve the morning newspaper, R.T. was standing on the sidewalk. He grinned at me and remarked, "Don't worry about an appeal, you were perfectly right to dismiss my application."

A few months later he moved, and I never found out whether he was being an understanding neighbour or buttering me up for the next time.

One law firm had obtained an injunction to prevent the competitor of their client from selling merchandise under a certain trade name. They then tried to trick the defendant into a breach of the injunction by sending phoney customers to his place of business who asked for that particular type of merchandise. Their client had conceived this subterfuge and the attorneys had gone along with the plan. Finally, they succeeded in inducing the defendant to make the sale, and they now sought a contempt citation for violation of the injunction. I was offended by the entire process and felt that the law firm had gone beyond the bounds of propriety. I stated my thoughts unequivocally to the attorney who was pleading the application and suggested that he request an adjournment and consult with his partners.

"What did we do wrong?" he asked. "We acted at all times on the instructions of the client."

"Mr. X," I observed, "when you dine with the devil you should use a long fork. Your fork wasn't long enough!"

That afternoon the senior partner of the firm appeared in Court and formally withdrew the contempt procedures.

Outside the palace the judge loses the aura of authority and trades the robes of office for the cloak of anonymity. Recognition by a witness or litigant can invite reactions ranging from surprise and curiosity to angry demands for an explanation. I cherish a few of the exclamations garnered at these sudden encounters.

"Look, he doesn't sleep in his gown!"

"I'm sorry, I didn't recognize you with clothes on."

"Oh my God, you're the last person I expected to meet!"

"You b —— d!"

On one such occasion I was confronted by a woman who looked vaguely familiar. "Oh, Judge Steinberg," she observed, "I was a witness in your court. You are just like Solomon."

I could not resist the urge to reply, "I trust that means I shall enjoy the love of one thousand women!"

Another time, my wife and I were in the video rental shop in Ste. Agathe looking for a movie when a young lady I didn't recognize ran over and threw her arms around my neck. She then proceeded to kiss me on the cheek and said, "Thank you for what you did for my sister."

Either she had embraced the wrong judge or I had done the right thing. I wish I knew who she and her sister were!

Chance meetings with attorneys are more informative. They frequently tell me in public places or even in the street that a document was filed, that a particular case was settled, or that a judgment was well or poorly received.

One Saturday, while standing in the neighbourhood bakery, I was approached by a slight, blonde woman, who addressed me by name. I looked at her intently but could not place her. Sensing my discomfort, she said, "I was in your office for a conference last month."

My lack of recall persisted, so I simply said, "I hope I treated you well!"

"Yes, you were perfectly right," she answered, "and next time I shall be better prepared."

One month my wife and I had friends from abroad staying with us, and we planned to meet during the noon break at a restaurant located one block from the courthouse.

That morning I was assigned a case in which an employer sought an injunction to prevent a former senior employee from competing with it after the termination of employment. The positions of the parties were described in the written documents and affidavits, and the hearing was limited to legal arguments by the attorneys.

In the style of the times, each lawyer presented me with a bound booklet of several hundred pages containing copies of the judgments and other authorities upon which he relied. The presentations were excellent.

During the morning coffee break I told my usher about my luncheon appointment and asked him to help me manoeuvre an extended lunch hour. I intended to create the illusion that I would eat a sandwich in my office and devote the lunch adjournment to the study of the written submissions. The usher placed a grocery cart near the courtroom. I instructed him on a signal, to push the cart into the courtroom and noisily gather and remove all the books and papers on my desk. The attorneys would think that I was studying their case during the lunch break.

The timing of events was perfect. At twelve-fifteen, when the final argument was concluded, I announced that I would review their written notes and arguments during the recess and render judgment later that afternoon. The recess would be longer than usual to enable me to read all the material submitted.

When the court adjourned, my usher escorted me out of the courtroom to the private elevator. He then re-entered the courtroom, solemnly pushing the grocery cart, and with great dignity and due deliberation, carefully loaded every book and paper from my desk into the cart. The loaded cart was left in the corridor adjacent to the courtroom.

In the meantime, I dashed into the judges' private elevator and left the building. Within four or five minutes, I reached the restaurant. By twelve-thirty, I was sitting with my wife and friends, sipping a glass of white wine. At twelve-forty the plaintiff, his attorney, and two associates entered the restaurant and were assigned the adjacent table. So much for the best-laid plans!

The judge's image is enhanced by a detailed dress code. Black and red gowns are worn when witnesses are present; on other occasions a dark grey jacket and striped pants are considered appropriate attire. One day when I was acting as a rover shifting between different courtrooms my first assignment had to do with a procedural matter, which meant that I did not need to wear the gown.

I was wearing a new dark grey blazer, and as tribute to the approaching summer, had placed a flower in my lapel. One of the attorneys, a young lady in her twenties, arrived early. She looked up at me and asked, "May I make a personal comment?"

Flattered and preening, I replied expectantly, "Yes?"

"My grandmother sends her regards," she said with a smile.

During the court recess, I phoned the senior partner of her firm to find out who she was. His reply was simply, "Don't you know Sarah Green's granddaughter?"

I know Sarah Green and will not forget her granddaughter's deflating remark!

Three times that morning I changed my attire and transferred to different courtrooms. When I received my fourth assignment that day from the clerk who coordinates the practice division, I bellowed into the phone, "Madam, this is the fourth time you have asked me to remove my clothes and proceed to a different room. This may be a palace, but I am not the royal courtesan!"

Judges tend to carry the formal dress habit into daily life. This was never so apparent as the day I met Natan Sharansky. Although physically small, he is a giant in the field of human rights. Throughout his long incarceration in a Soviet prison, he retained his dignity, courage, and a sense of humour. His ultimate release and emigration from the Soviet Union was attributable to the efforts of many human rights activists. Perhaps the most decisive and influential was his lawyer, Professor Irwin Cotler of McGill University. The briefs submitted on behalf of his client are a model of comprehensiveness and originality.

Several months following his release, Natan Sharansky was invited to deliver the inaugural lecture in the human rights program that bears his name at McGill University, and I was among the fortunate who were invited to lunch with him privately before the lecture.

That morning, I was sitting in practice court wearing the usual rather formal attire — striped pants, white shirt, and a dark grey jacket. I managed to finish the morning's docket quickly and arrived at the McGill Faculty Club ten minutes early. To delay, I wandered into the men's room, where I happened upon the guest of honour standing in a corner. He was wearing only underpants, stockings, and shoes. Professor Cotler was standing beside him like a valet holding two pairs of pants and other clothing. Unperturbed and unflappable, Professor Cotler said, "Natan, may I present Mr. Justice Henry Steinberg of the Superior Court. Henry, this is Natan Sharansky. Unfortunately Natan's airplane was delayed and he did not have an opportunity to change his clothes for today's luncheon."

As we shook hands, the door to the washroom opened and Philip Vineberg, Q.C., then one of Canada's outstanding corporate lawyers, entered. He was formally dressed in a dark blue suit and white shirt. Once again, Professor Cotler, the consummate gentleman, presented the small, semi-naked guest of honour.

"Natan, please meet Mr. Philip Vineberg, Q.C., a former head of the Bar Society of Montreal and one of the outstanding members of this community. Phil, may I present Natan Sharansky."

As Phil Vineberg shook hands with the guest, the incongruity of the situation became overbearing. Both Phil and I blushed and retreated from the washroom to leave Sharansky in peace. As the door closed behind us, we could hear his polite inquiry, "Professor Cotler, is there anyone else in this bathroom that you want me to meet?"

Among the Canadian provinces, Quebec alone adheres to the civil law system. History and determination have assured that the private law of Quebec remains faithful to its French origins, while the rest of Canada evolved under the common law system that prevails in most countries settled by English-speaking peoples.

One feature of the civil law is that certain legal transactions are handled by public officials known as notaries, rather than by lawyers. They trace their origins to the time of the

Crusades, when King Louis IX of France invested thirty-six individuals with the power to preside at the signing of certain important documents in order to ensure their authenticity, validity, and compliance with the requirements of the parties concerned. In Quebec, the agreements that must be received or executed in the presence of a notary include mortgages, marriage contracts, and certain renunciations of rights. Notaries obtain a degree in law from a recognized university and follow certain prescribed additional courses before they are admitted to the profession. As public officers, they take the oath of office in the presence of a judge of the Superior Court.

One day, one such notary-to-be called my office. "This is Louise Sancerre," she said. "I believe you know my father, Samuel Sancerre. He said I should call and you could help me. I have just completed the notarial course and am unable to attend the formal ceremonies."

"Yes," I responded, frantically searching my memory in an unsuccessful attempt to picture Samuel Sancerre. I recalled neither the name nor an image. "What exactly can I do?"

"Under the terms of the Notarial Code, only a Superior Court justice can administer the oath of office. Since I won't be able to attend the formal ceremony, I ask you to receive my parents and me in your Chambers and administer the oath to me privately."

"It would be my pleasure. I suggest you come to my office Friday morning at about ten."

"Yes, that would be fine."

"My office is on the fifteenth floor, and there is a small box near the door to the private quarters where you will find my name. Just push the button and my secretary will admit you."

"Thank you, sir," she said, and hung up.

For the remainder of the week, I tried without success to remember Samuel Sancerre. In the meantime, I located the Notarial Code among the Revised Statutes of Quebec and studied the relevant sections. I also made sure that the Bible given me at my own swearing-in would be conveniently located on a shelf back of my desk.

On Friday morning, I dressed with care; I wanted to look the role I was about to play. As I prepared, the missing name and face of Samuel Sancerre continued to intrigue me. I asked my secretary to watch for their arrival and admit them without the lengthy interrogation and scrutiny she forces on unexpected intruders whom she perceives as a threat to her leisurely Friday morning pace.

At precisely ten o'clock, the buzzer rang. I heard voices in the exterior office and rose to greet Louise and her parents at the door to my private office. Louise was a typical college student: young, attractive, and intense. She resembled the many young friends of my own children. Samuel and his wife were considerably older than I expected. They appeared to be in their sixties, were small and frail, and spoke English with an eastern European accent. I could not recall if I had met or spoken to either of them in the past.

I made a small speech about the importance of the notarial profession and my long association with many of its members over the years. Then I reached for the Bible, instructed Louise to place her right hand on it, and read the oath. Her parents looked on quietly.

"So help you God," I concluded. I congratulated Louise and her parents and personally ushered them to the outer corridor.

I did not give the incident any further thought until two weeks later when I read in the obituary columns that Samuel Sancerre had died and that the burial had taken place in the cemetery of the synagogue that I attend. I called the Rabbi for more information about the deceased.

Samuel Sancerre was of Polish origin. He had fled his native country at the outbreak of World War II and entered France, where he changed his name from Schwartz to Sancerre. After the war, he and his wife emigrated to Canada.

Louise, their only child, was born late in life, and Samuel had dreamt of the day his only child would graduate from university and become a professional. He had been ill for the past year, but the strength that enabled him to survive the rigor and horrors of war served him again in the final months of his life, as he struggled to remain alive until his only child, Notary Louise Sancerre, took her oath of office.

That swearing-in was more poignant than I had realized. The Sancerre episode was a preparation, in some sense, as the following year, my son Sandy graduated from law school and completed the additional notarial studies. He announced to the family that the formal oath taking would take place at a ceremony to be held in one of Montreal's major hotels. The year's 197 successful candidates would all attend.

The arrangements made by the Order of Notaries permitted each candidate to invite three guests to witness the ceremony, but that meant we would be short one ticket. My wife and I, Sandy's wife, and our other son all wanted to attend.

The problem was not insoluble, however. After all, judicial office has its perquisites. I phoned the office of the Chief Justice to find out who would preside at the ceremony, and his secretary told me that the Chief always performed the honours personally. I wrote a note to the Chief that should it prove inconvenient for him to attend this year's swearing-in of the new notaries, I should be honoured to replace him.

Within a day, he phoned my office.

"Why did you send me that note?" he inquired with his habitual forthrightness.

"Well," I answered, "this year my son Sandy is among the candidates who will be taking the oath, and . . . "

"Would you like to replace me?"

"Absolutely not," I answered. "I was told you preside at the ceremony each year, and I wish you to continue to do so until the age of one hundred and twenty. However, if, through unforeseen circumstances, you are unable to preside at the ceremonies, I request the honour of replacing you."

"Right. Have a good day."

That week, I presided at the criminal jury trial in Joliette about forty miles away. When I returned to the palace, I discovered several letters. The first was a formal invitation from the Board of Notaries to the Chief Justice requesting his attendance at the ceremony. There was a copy of his acknowledgement and expression of regret that he was obliged on that day to hear an application that could not be postponed or referred to another judge, and the suggestion that he designate me as his representative. Finally, there was a letter from the Board of Notaries addressed to me, opining that they were "ravished" and honoured by the thought that I would be available to administer the oath of office to this year's successful applicants. I immediately phoned the secretary of the board to advise her that I, too, was "ravished" because my son was among the new notaries who would be taking the oath.

The following day, the board delivered to my office a history of the notarial profession, suitably inscribed in commemoration of my participation in the ceremony at which my son would assume his responsibilities as a notary, together with a suggestion as to the content of my speech. Speech? I hadn't realized I would have to make a speech.

"You and your bright ideas," my secretary muttered.

"Not only do I have to type your judgments, which are too long anyway, but now I have to attend to your personal affairs and speeches."

"Don't complain," I responded. "It's only a five-minute speech, and I promise not to do more than three drafts."

"Okay," she answered, "but I am doing this for your son and your wife, not for you. I suppose you will speak in French. Your son will appreciate my corrections to your speech. His spoken French is better than yours. His accent is also better."

"I know, I know," I muttered as I returned to my private office.

Realizing that I would be speaking to 197 new notaries, the officers of the board, and approximately 600 invited guests, as well as certain dignitaries, including the Deputy Minister of Justice, I worked hard on my few comments. There must have been ten drafts of those seven pages, each of which was subject to correction by my secretary. In the end, I'm sure the corrections were more appreciated than the comments.

The day before the ceremony, I received a phone call from the secretary of the Board of Notaries, "*Monsieur le juge*, we are delighted that you will preside at the ceremony and administer the oath to the new notaries. However, there is one small problem."

I waited expectantly as she continued, "Section 221 of the Courts of Justice Act precludes your administering the oath to members of your immediate family. Naturally, we have no objection, but what if your son's credentials are to be subsequently challenged, and . . . "

"Say no more. I shall do the correct thing," I replied.

My speech was received with great enthusiasm, and afterwards, I administered the oath to 196 young notaries with dignity and warmth. It was an outstanding ceremony. Unfortunately, my son Sandy was unable to participate. He took the oath in the office of my colleague, Irving Halperin, in the presence of my secretary and me. "You and your bright ideas," she said. "I hope they don't invite you back next year!"

Such are the perquisites of the judiciary.

8

Lawyers:
The Long, the Short,
and the Tall

Lawyers are essential participants in the legal process. They are its managers and creatures. Their stature is dependent on the public's perception and the effectiveness of the system of justice. Lawyers come in all sizes, two sexes, many configurations, and with varying talents and skills. There is no perfect combination. Ruthless, aggressive personalities do not always prevail. The meek can inherit success.

The received wisdom is that no litigant should represent himself. The lawyer who represents himself, in the well-known phrase, has a fool for a client and a knave for a lawyer; and the non-lawyer who pleads his own case is equally foolish. Judges confronted with those who have chosen to make their own defence will implore and encourage parties to retain counsel and inform them of available legal aid facilities. In the absence of counsel, the judge must either witness the

111

exploitation of the unrepresented party or act as judge and counsel simultaneously. Both offend his sense of justice, impair his partiality, and, more seriously, may distort the result.

Justice Pierre Michaud was presented with such a situation. He looked down at the plaintiff and inquired, "Sir, do you have an attorney representing you in this case?"

"The Lord Almighty will plead on my behalf," replied the plaintiff.

"May I suggest," continued the judge, "that you engage local counsel to assist as well."

At a pre-trial conference held in my office, the plaintiff represented himself, though the defendant was represented by counsel.

"Sir," I advised him, "you must engage an attorney."

"Why?" he responded, clutching a Civil Code. "I know the law."

"Sir," I continued, "you would not operate on yourself after having read Gray's *Anatomy*, you would not pull your own tooth, and you should not be your own attorney. Please hire a lawyer!"

"It's not necessary."

"Sir, you are going to lose your case."

"Why do you say that?" he asked.

"Because I have read the file. Please obtain advice from a lawyer."

"It's not necessary. You have told me your opinion and you are a judge."

"Sir, I have not heard the witness and only gave you a preliminary opinion based on a quick perusal of the file."

"What good will an attorney do if I am going to lose?"

"He may help you to settle your case or present it in a better light."

"I refuse to hire a lawyer. I know all about law and lawyers. What should I do?"

"Go settle your case for $3,000."

"Mister Judge, why would anyone pay me $3,000 if I am going to lose?"

"Because this case will last three days and the defendant will pay $1,000 a day to avoid being in court with you."

"How can you know he will pay the $3,000?"

"I don't know. I guessed and was correct. Look at his attorney sitting beside you and nodding his head."

"I think you're wrong and I shall win. Please fix the trial date."

I fixed the trial date. He subsequently pleaded his own case and lost. He complained that the presiding judge had failed to study the matter adequately. The reasoned, eighteen-page judgment was ultimately confirmed by the Court of Appeal, where, as you may have guessed, the plaintiff represented himself.

In the majority of cases pleaded by competent attorneys, the result will be substantially the same, no matter who acts as counsel. In some cases, however, the ability of the litigator, and the personality, insight, and scholarship of the advocate will affect the outcome.

Lawyers live in a constant state of tension between the competing demands of clients, their responsibility as officers of the court, and the constraints of the law. Good lawyers listen to a client, analyze the problem, determine the appropriate course of action, and then seek to convince the client and the judge of its correctness. Their intellectual arsenal must contain erudition, logic, discretion, courage, and a sense of humour. The trial lawyer needs strong nerves and the ability to cope with the unexpected.

Lawyer Gerald Tremblay was once pleading for the issue of an injunction before Justice Landry. Clutching a booklet containing photocopies of judgments of the Court of Appeal, he read from a leading opinion of Mr. Justice Owen of that court. As he turned the page, he noticed that his secretary had inadvertently copied the same page twice. Without flinching, he continued, "And Mr. Justice Owen considered this matter so important that he repeated it a second time, in identical terms on the following page. . . ."

The court also has its moments of comic farce. Lawyer François Messier, known for his eloquence and elegance, is not above a good joke all the same. On one occasion he was lead counsel for some plaintiffs who claimed extra fees for the construction of a sewage disposal plant. He had asked the witness a seemingly innocuous question and was surprised when the defendant's attorney objected. Messier lifted his head in mock pain and embarrassment. He stared first at me and then turned to the witness and asked, "Do you object to my question?"

The witness shook his head from side to side. He then asked every one of his four co-counsels for the plaintiffs the same question. Each shook his head and replied, "No." Finally, he turned to the audience and went through the same exercise with several of the spectators who were obviously officers and employees of the plaintiffs. After completing this informal poll, Messier addressed me, "My lord, it is obvious that the only person in the room who objects to my asking the question is the attorney for the defendant. I think the objection should be dismissed."

When I dismissed the objection, even the attorney for the defendant joined in the general laughter.

A lawyer rushing down the emergency stairway one day happened upon a gentleman hurriedly mounting the stairs backwards. He thought nothing of the strange sight until fifteen minutes later when he entered the courtroom and found himself pleading before the gentleman he had encountered climbing the stairs. To this day he is convinced that his case was heard by a judge who had taken leave of his senses.

How could he know that Mr. Justice X is an avid skier who was simply doing the ankle- and leg-strengthening exercises prescribed by his ski instructor?

Joking about serious matters in court is generally unwise, but the absurdities surrounding trivial details and administrative matters make up for the seriousness of the cases.

One year during the week before Easter, I was listening to a lengthy case that could not be completed that week and would require an additional day of trial. On Friday afternoon, I explained to the lawyers that I wanted to complete the trial as quickly as possible and would be available to hear them any time the following week. The attorneys reached for their agendas and started commenting to me and to each other how each of them was busy on Monday, Tuesday, Wednesday, and Thursday. When I politely suggested that the following Friday might be suitable, one of the attorneys observed, "Your Lordship, if we proceed next Friday, you will be the first judge to sit that day since Pontius Pilate."

On another occasion when it was obvious that the matter could not be completed that day, I sought to obtain agreement on a later date for the hearing.

"Gentlemen," I said. "I note that we are approaching the noon hour. For the convenience of both you and your witnesses, I suggest that we agree on a schedule for the continuation of this hearing. I estimate we shall require this afternoon and one further complete day."

"My lord," began Lawyer P, "I would be most appreciative if you would hear us tomorrow and if we could finish before tomorrow night. Quite honestly, I have reservations to fly to the Carribean the following day. If this is not possible, I shall of course cancel my vacation plans. Should that become necessary, I shall be here in court, but my heart will be in Trinidad."

"I have no heart," Lawyer F interjected.

"I would also request," continued Lawyer P, "that we start

the afternoon sessions at 2:00 P.M. instead of 2:15 P.M. and thereby gain an additional half-hour, if the Court approves."

Lawyer F was on his feet in an instant. "My lord, I have no objection to proceeding tomorrow, the next day, or any other day, but the shortened lunch hour recess is not convenient because I have an appointment to meet a client at the St. Amable Restaurant."

"I understand, Mr. F," I observed curtly. "You have a stomach but no heart! The Court will adjourn to 2:15 in the afternoon. The Court will sit tomorrow, and there will be a short lunchtime adjournment tomorrow. Between now and then, I suggest you find a way to restrain your appetite."

Another time, Lawyer F was before me during a lengthy trial. While cross-examining the witness, he sought to compensate for his diminutive height by being aggressive. Here is the transcript:

Lawyer K: My lord, . . . I would again ask Mr. F to please not stand on top of the witness.

Lawyer F: I'm not on top of the witness, my lord. The witness is about two feet taller than me. It's been a continuous regret that I do not have the extra foot of height.

The Witness: I'm sorry for you, Mr. F.

Lawyer F: However, there is not much that I can do about it, my lord. I belong to a family of genes that have small growth.

The Court: You will just have to live with your problem, Mr. F.

Lawyer F: I know, my lord.

Although they can have a reputation for being uptight, lawyers may use humour when no logical explanation is available. When one case was called three times and the plaintiff did not appear, his attorney finally rose to her feet and explained, "My lord, my client was here earlier today. While we were waiting in the corridor, I reviewed his testimony with him. My questions were so realistic he must have thought the trial was finished and gone home!"

I also relish the memory of the moment when an attorney asked the following introductory question during a custody hearing, "Would you tell the Court how your child was conceived?"

And then there was the lawyer suffering from inverted syntax, who asked a witness, "Is that woman the only wife you have living in your house?"

Sam, a specialist in labour and administrative law, shuffles his three hundred pounds about the palace like a battleship brushing aside a school of tuna. The first time he appeared before me, he represented the owner of a seedy restaurant that had fired a nude dancer. The young lady in question saw her dismissal as an opportunity to change careers and sought an alternative vocation. After six weeks of searching, she succeeded in obtaining a secretarial position. She then presented a grievance against her former employer for unjustified dismissal and claimed her lost salary for the preceding six weeks.

The claim was maintained by a labour arbitrator. Sam presented an application to the Superior Court, asserting that the arbitrator did not understand the theory of mitigation of damages, that the employee could have obtained alternate employment as a nude dancer the day following her dismissal, and that the lost salary for six weeks was as a result of her decision to change her profession and was not a consequence of the unjustified dismissal. I dismissed the application and left town for two weeks the following day.

Upon my return, I found a phone message from Sam, which I returned immediately.

"Sam, what's the problem?"

"Judge, do you remember the judgment you rendered in the case of the nude dancer?"

"Yes."

"During your absence, I received the written version of your judgment, and it contains a serious mistake."

"Sam, as you know, I've been out of town for several weeks. I assume that it was typed by a court stenographer and signed by one of the clerks. But perhaps I can help. What is the nature of the mistake?"

"Judge, the typist transposed the names of the attorneys and the parties. The official written version describes *me* dancing nude on the tables in a restaurant!"

Perhaps Sam is just accident-prone. Months later I met him in the corridor in front of the office of the Chief Justice.

"Sam, what are you doing here today?" I asked.

"You won't believe this one," he replied. "Last month I pleaded a case and the judge reserved judgment. A week later, I received a call from the judge's secretary asking me to come to his office later, along with my opponent. When we entered his office, he pointed to an envelope on his desk which bore the name and return address of my client. The judge opened the envelope in our presence. It contained $2,000 cash. I don't know what to do now. I'm meeting the Chief Justice in a few minutes."

"Sam," I said, "without knowing any more about the case, it sounds as if your client may be guilty of contempt of court."

"Contempt?" he responded. "I'd settle for contempt. I'm afraid he'll be charged with bribery."

I placed my arm on his shoulder: "Sam, $2,000 used to be bribery. But if you take inflation into account, it's only contempt!"

Most attorneys who appear before me are hardworking, highly competent professionals fully aware of their responsibilities to their clients and to the law. A handful, however, are disappointing.

Each Wednesday the team of judges assigned to hear long civil trials meets to distribute the week's cases. The "captain" of the team reviews the files and provides the list of these cases, as well as any unusual details. Assignments are chosen on the basis of seniority and schedule requirements. A judge may decline a file because of a close relationship with an attorney or a party involved, dislike of the subject matter, or conflict of interest. Most prefer cases with a predictable duration; few seek marathon trials that will last more than two months. Naturally, the junior members of the team have the most restricted choice.

The distribution meeting I attended was routine. Each case seemed predictable as to duration and difficulty until our captain remarked, "There is only one small change on the list of cases that I distributed yesterday. In *Ortex* versus *Morimport*, Robert Bochatz will represent the defendant, Morimport. . . ." As I said, most attorneys are hardworking, competent, and logical. Bochatz is the exception to the rule. He inhabits a world of his own illusions, whose logic is known only to him, a world where the rules of law were repealed and elementary courtesy vanished long ago. He is a schlemiel who combines the personality and stability of Roger Rabbit with the character of Captain Hook.

Audible groans escaped the lips of several judges. "Is that the fellow who was disbarred last year?" "Is he the one who's always late and never prepared?" "Did the bar reinstate him?"

"That's him. This is a claim for unpaid shipments of shirts and blouses from the Orient. Mr. Bochatz called my office to announce that he will file a counterclaim for damages alleging problems of sizes, colours, and delays in deliveries. The trial was originally fixed for three days. Even that is a long time, but since the plaintiff, Ortex, is a Hong Kong trading company, some witnesses will testify in Chinese and require interpreters. There will be a question of forged documents such as delivery slips and bills of lading. I won't schedule any other cases for the judge who accepts this assignment. Because of the change of attorneys, it now falls into the unpredictable duration category."

I looked around the room. Heads were nodding from side to side, two judges wrote a large "*non*" in the margin opposite the case, and the only person in the room who was junior to me blanched visibly.

"Lise," I said to her, "give me the file. I managed to survive a pre-trial conference with him and I think I can control the situation."

"Good luck, and thanks. If you have a problem, call me. And above all, don't lose your temper."

"I won't." The file was shoved along the table in my direction. Most of the judges grinned; a few sighed in relief. Hopefully this sacrifice would earn me a choice assignment at the next distribution meeting.

"Lise, I want the case fixed for room 15.10. It's a double size courtroom close to my office, so I'll have a place to wait for Bochatz in comfort during the breaks."

"Okay. Anything else?"

"Well, if you have any influence with Rocket, perhaps you can convince him to outfit the room with a double whirlpool bath and TV."

At nine o'clock Monday morning, my usher, Linda, entered the office and handed me a cup of coffee.

"*Monsieur le juge,*" she asked with a smile, "have we an interesting case this week?"

"No, we have an interesting lawyer, Robert Bochatz. I managed to get the big room opposite my office. Finish your coffee, then walk down and look into the courtroom. I want to begin on time if possible."

She returned at nine-thirty to inform me that everyone was present, except Bochatz.

"Ask the clerk to note his absence in the record and to call Bochatz on the loudspeaker every ten minutes until he arrives. Let me know what happens."

At twenty after ten, Linda reappeared at my office door and smiled. "Mr. Bochatz has arrived and he looks pale."

"Let's go." I rose, put on my gown, and followed her through the corridor. As she pressed the buzzer and announced, "All rise," I stepped rapidly into the courtroom, nodded to the clerk, and listened to the announcement that the court was now open. Robert Bochatz gave me a weak smile.

"Good morning, my lord."

"Good morning, Mr. Bochatz."

"I may have to ask the indulgence of the Court throughout this trial," he continued. "I have not been feeling well and may request an adjournment from time to time. I was unable to sleep last night. That's why I am late today."

"I understand. Any time you do not feel well, just advise me and the Court will adjourn for as long as you request."

"I vomited all night," he volunteered.

Why did he have to say that? I hadn't asked for details. I had agreed to his request and now for the rest of the trial I would have trouble erasing the image of Bochatz in a bathrobe, wandering about his house in the early hours of the morning, sick to his stomach and retching. Oh well, on with the case. I turned to Robin Pratt, who was acting for Ortex.

"Mr. Pratt, does the plaintiff wish to make any opening remarks?"

"Yes, my lord," he answered, "but first I wish to express my appreciation to Mr. Bochatz for attending and proceeding despite personal indisposition.

"The plaintiff, Ortex Trading, seeks the sum of $249,000 from the defendant, Morimport Limited. During the past four years, Albert Morrison, the president of Morimport Limited, made frequent trips to Hong Kong, where he purchased thousands of dozens of blouses, shirts, T-shirts, and sweaters. Ortex arranged for the manufacture of these products in China and their shipment to Canada. It was agreed that when the shipments arrived at Canada Customs, Morimport would go to the offices of the Hong Kong Bank of Canada, pay for the shipment, and pick up the customs and shipping documents. Then Morimport would take these documents to the customs warehouse and take delivery of the blouses and shirts shipped. In certain cases, Mr. Albert Morrison ignored the bank, made no payments to Ortex, and obtained the shipments from the customs warehouse by presenting forged documents. Morimport then sold the blouses and shirts and kept the money. Ortex claims the value of shipments for which payment was not made."

"Thank you, Mr. Pratt. Please proceed with your case."

The first day was slow and uneventful. A succession of witnesses explained the system of manufacturing, packaging, and shipping the merchandise, and the related banking transactions. Several of the witnesses spoke Chinese only and were questioned through an official interpreter. Bochatz remained quiet throughout and furiously scribbled in his yellow notepad. He declined to cross-examine the witnesses despite the continued and agitated whispering of his client. Four or five times, I granted his requests for brief adjournments. Matters were proceeding better and faster than I had anticipated. The plaintiff's evidence would be completed the next day.

On Tuesday morning, Robert Bochatz was late again. He was summoned on the loudspeaker system at nine-thirty and at successive ten-minute intervals, until a quarter after ten, when he made his appearance.

"Mr. Bochatz, I trust you are feeling better this morning," I commented.

"Oh yes, my lord."

"Well, perhaps you can explain to your colleague, to your client, and to me why you are forty minutes late."

"It's my car. As you know, there was a snowfall overnight. I don't have snow tires on my car and I had trouble getting out of the driveway. I wanted to put the snow tires on last night, but the garage was busy and I had to prepare this case . . . "

I gestured with my hand. "Enough, Mr. Bochatz. Would you please do whatever is necessary to ensure that you are in court on time tomorrow morning."

"I promise . . . "

Turning to Robin Pratt, I said, "Mr. Pratt, would you proceed."

"Yes, my lord."

The morning session was devoted to the completion of the plaintiff's evidence. Once again Bochatz made copious notes, remained silent, and refrained from cross-examining the witnesses. At noon when Pratt announced that his proof was complete, Bochatz stood and smiled.

"My lord," he said, "my client doesn't deny that the plaintiff shipped merchandise having a value of $249,000, for which it was not paid. Of course, they did. It was not necessary for these witnesses to come from Hong Kong and I hope you will not order payment of their travel expense as part of the court costs. However, the plaintiff should not be paid because the sizes were all wrong, the colours in the boxes were all mixed up, and Morimport's customers refused to accept these shipments until the price was reduced. I have here a folder of documents, letters, shipping memos, and credit notes, which prove . . . "

Robin Pratt was on his feet. "My lord, I object. The Rules provide that all documents under the control of a party and intended to be used at trial must be filed in advance so that the opposing party may consult them. It is apparent that Mr.

Bochatz intends to file that bag full of documents without notice and contrary to the Rules of Procedure."

Bochatz casually turned over the large, red envelope and emptied hundreds of assorted papers onto the table in front of the Court clerk. A number floated to the floor. Bochatz knelt, then he retrieved and added them to the paper mountain on the table. The Court clerk was bewildered, Robin Pratt's face reddened, and four Chinese gentlemen seated in the audience peered intently, uncomprehending, at the papers. Robert Bochatz smiled innocently and continued.

"Morimport is a new client. They transferred this file to me last month. I phoned the judge in charge of long-duration cases and informed her that I would be making a counterclaim. She said that I should present the application to the trial judge. I now ask you for permission to file the counterclaim and produce these supporting documents."

"My lord, my lord, I object," exploded Robin Pratt. "This is unfair and contrary to the Rules of Procedure."

I glanced towards the corner, where Linda was seated, a handkerchief clutched to her nose to conceal a smile. Well, I had promised her an interesting lawyer and she would not be disappointed.

Turning back, I said, "Mr. Bochatz, it would have been appropriate to make this request at the beginning of the trial and not try to ambush or take your colleague by surprise. You place the Court in a difficult position. If I grant your request to make a counterclaim at this time, the plaintiff may be prejudiced. On the other hand, to refuse your application could result in a denial of the defendant's rights."

Bochatz's smile vanished. He assumed the air of a child about to be punished for a reason he could not comprehend. His eyes turned watery as I continued. "As for these papers you have dumped on the table, we have rules for the production of documents. They must be sorted and filed in a logical sequence. Copies must be given to your opponent in advance."

"I know, I know," he explained, "but my client just sent these papers to me. If you only knew the trouble I have had preparing this case. My client's affairs are a mess."

At this point Albert Morrison interjected. "I gave you everything you asked for."

Bochatz turned towards his client and asked, "How many times did I have to call you? Why were some papers only delivered to me yesterday?"

"Because your office was closed last week," Morrison answered.

"Well, I was pleading an important case and I was sick."

"My case is important too."

"I know, I know, but . . ."

"Gentlemen, gentlemen," I interjected. "Please remember you are on the same side. You are attorney and client. Now stop bickering!"

Looking at both attorneys, I continued, "Gentlemen, I have decided to permit the filing of the counterclaim and the production of the documents. Mr. Bochatz, I order you, during the luncheon recess, to prepare two photocopies of every document you wish to produce, one for me and one for your opponent and put these documents and papers in some order. Mr. Pratt, I realize your position. Please review this matter with your clients during the recess. We can continue with the trial this afternoon, or, if you request an adjournment to a later date, I shall direct the defendant to put the file in order and the trial will resume at the earliest moment my schedule permits. I shall be guided by your suggestion. The Court is adjourned until three o'clock this afternoon."

Linda called, "All rise," and led me back to the office. "*Monsieur le juge*," she said, "I shall return for a moment to observe the courtroom. I will see you at ten to three."

"Fine, *bon appétit!*" I called after her.

Just before three o'clock, Linda appeared at my office door. "*Monsieur le juge*, unlike the other attorneys, Mr. Bochatz does not change into his court outfit downstairs in the locker room. He brings a gown in his briefcase, pulls it out at the last minute, and puts it on as you enter the room.

"After you adjourned for lunch today, he gathered his papers to make photocopies and left the courtroom wearing his gown and carrying his briefcase. The clerk did not notice the winter coat on a chair in the back of the room and locked the door, so Monsieur Bochatz could not retrieve his coat at lunchtime. Well, Marie and I ate lunch across the street at McDonalds today, and you can imagine my surprise when I saw Monsieur Bochatz wearing his gown and carrying a briefcase and ordering a Big Mac. The people in the restaurant all stared and laughed."

"Did you offer to sit with him?"

"*Mais non!* It is sufficient that I sit quietly in court and listen to him all day. When we return to court, you may notice his gown is wet from the snow."

"Thank you, Linda. Are they ready for me to return?"

"I believe so."

As I had expected, Robin Pratt chose to continue the trial. "My lord," he announced, "I have reviewed this matter with my clients and we wish to continue. The cost of bringing people from Hong Kong and the disruption caused by their absence is substantial. Another delay will increase these costs."

"Thank you. Mr. Bochatz, did you make the required copies?"

"Yes, my lord."

"Proceed!"

"I must request a further adjournment. I spent my lunchtime making the copies and was obliged to eat a hurried lunch at McDonald's."

"Yes, so I understand."

"I did not have time to discuss certain matters with my client and must now ask for fifteen minutes."

"Mr. Bochatz, you strain the Court's patience. Nonetheless, I shall grant your request."

When court resumed, Albert Morrison was called as a witness. His testimony was confused. I relaxed and listened but did not understand the unending array of invoices, statements, and memos which had no relationship to each other or to the case before me. Twice I adjourned the Court for periods of ten minutes so that Bochatz and his client could sort the papers out.

Just after four, a bicycle courier, wearing the usual tight jeans, leather jacket, and carrying a telephone and crash helmet, entered the courtroom. Bochatz stopped in mid-question, accepted an envelope, and read its contents. Then he rushed toward the door in pursuit of the messenger. As the double doors to the public corridor closed, I stared at the startled Morrison and the seated attorney for the plaintiff and imploded. For a fleeting second, I considered whether rudeness was equivalent to contempt. Then I dismissed the thought, rose slowly, and announced, "The Court will adjourn until nine-thirty tomorrow morning so as to permit counsel sufficient time to consult his messenger service."

As I left the courtroom, the door closed behind me and I could hear the returning Bochatz ask his client, "What happened? Where's the judge?"

At nine-thirty the next morning, Bochatz was not present. Enough was enough. I instructed Linda to open the Court, entered, and sat quietly waiting. Ten minutes later he arrived, out of breath. As his coat slid to the floor, he extracted a creased gown from his briefcase, rushed to the front of the courtroom, and explained, "My car wouldn't start. I would have been here on time, but my engine was frozen."

"Mr. Bochatz," I said, "the temperature outside is above freezing. How do you expect me to believe your excuse?"

"That's just the problem," he replied. "How could I have

expected my engine to freeze when the temperature was above thirty-two degrees?"

Bochatz spent the morning reviewing the papers and inviting Albert Morrison to explain them. The air was heavy and I made a special effort to concentrate on his testimony. I developed a headache and was grateful when noon arrived. Upon entering the private washroom adjacent to my office, I noticed a stenographer's chair beside the toilet. Perhaps the trial, the poor ventilation, and the headache were causing my mind to play tricks. I took a Tylenol and glanced again at the silent toilet and steno chair. There could be no rational explanation. Some things are best ignored. I went for a long walk at lunchtime. Perhaps the fresh air would clear my head. When I returned an hour later, my headache had disappeared, but the mysterious steno chair remained. I casually walked over to Jacqueline's desk and inquired, "Is everything well today?"

"*Oui, Monsieur le juge,*" she responded.

"Are you missing something?" I asked.

"*Non,* why do you ask?"

"Well," I continued, "something strange is happening in my office. Have you looked into the private washroom?"

"*Oui.*"

"Did you notice anything different? Anything added?"

"*Non.*"

"Did you not observe a steno chair beside the toilet?"

"Oh, yes," she replied breezily.

"Has the government's financial situation deteriorated to the point where soon they will be placing secretaries' chairs in the bathrooms and typewriters on the toilets?"

"Of course not. Why do you ask such a question?"

"Because," I said, " I cannot comprehend why there is a steno chair in my private washroom."

"We are hiding it there until the new bookcase is delivered," she announced.

"You are hiding a steno chair in my private washroom until a new bookcase is delivered? This is about as logical as the evidence presented by Robert Bochatz. I cannot endure more confusion. Please tell me slowly why there is a steno chair in my private washroom."

"*Monsieur le juge,*" she explained, "four months ago, Judge Halperin ordered a new bookcase. Well, they made a mistake and sent him two bookcases. Rocket would not admit the mistake and Judge Halperin must keep both of them, but they would not fit in his office. He has offered one to you and I accepted on your behalf. Rocket agreed."

"Thank you, but what about the steno chair?" I asked.

"Well," she continued, "Debby had ordered a new chair at the same time and received two. She did not need the extra chair and gave it to me as a gift. I am afraid that Rocket will see the extra chair when he visits to inspect the new bookcase, so I hid the chair in your washroom until the inspection is complete. Do you mind?"

"No, I do not mind, but next time please tell me in advance," I replied.

"I knew you would understand. Would you like some tea before court resumes?"

"Yes, thank you."

I sipped my tea slowly.

When I returned to court, Robert Bochatz declared that the examination in chief of Albert Morrison had been concluded.

"Thank you," I said.

"We will now proceed with the cross-examination of Mr. Morrison."

The contradictions and omissions became readily apparent during the cross-examination.

"Would you explain to the Court why the invoices for January 1987 do not appear on the statement for January 1987?"

Before the witness could answer, Bochatz rose and said, "I object."

"Why?" I asked.

"I already told the Court that the papers were a mess," he answered.

"Mr. Bochatz, please be seated and allow your client to answer the question." He squinted and sat down.

"Your Honour, may I request an adjournment?" the witness asked. "My nose is starting to bleed."

"The Court will adjourn for fifteen minutes."

Fifteen minutes later when the Court resumed, Linda placed a box of Kleenex before the witness. Bochatz began to squint some more, the questioning resumed, and Morrison answered from the depths of his Kleenex. Several other irrelevant objections were rapidly dismissed. When the day ended I announced, "The Court will resume at nine-thirty tomorrow and the punctual attendance of counsel will be appreciated."

Bochatz rose to his feet, looked up, and said, "My lord, this case was scheduled for three days. I do not know if I am available to continue tomorrow."

"Mr. Bochatz," I sighed, "you have been late for three consecutive days. You filed documents at the last moment and went for a stroll with your bicycle courier in the middle of this trial. Any additional days of trial are surely attributable to you. The trial will continue tomorrow and I suggest you owe it to your client to be present."

"Yes," murmured Albert Morrison through the Kleenex that he clutched to his nose. Robert Bochatz nodded in agreement.

Bochatz's punctual arrival on Thursday morning augured well for the rest of the trial. The cross-examination was concluded and arguments began. Robin Pratt was brief. The defendant had received the shipments and failed to make the payments at the bank. The plaintiff's claim was proven. I turned to Bochatz.

"You have admitted these facts. On what basis do you ask for the dismissal of the action? Undoubtedly you realize that once the admission is made, the burden of proof shifts and your client must convince the Court by preponderance of proof that the counterclaim is well founded. Do you think that the evidence you have presented would convince any reasonable man?"

"No, my lord," replied Bochatz. "I would not be convinced either. But I told you about the trouble I had getting information from my client." Then, turning to Morrison, he said, "I told you I needed more documents, didn't I?!"

"I gave you what I had," replied Morrison.

"Mr. Bochatz," I asked, "since you have not even convinced yourself, let alone the Court, do you wish to withdraw the counterclaim?"

"I shall ask my client," he answered.

"Don't ask me," remarked Morrison. "It's a legal question and you're the lawyer!"

"No, my lord, I will not withdraw the claim and I have a further submission to make."

"Yes, Mr. Bochatz."

"I wish to re-amend the counterclaim. Since you are not satisfied that there is a valid defence to the claim under the contract for the sale of textile products, I wish to amend the claim and request the cancellation of the contract itself."

"I am not quite sure I understand your request. If you ask for cancellation of the contract, you must offer to return the merchandise purchased. You cannot do so because Mr. Morrison testified it was sold to third parties."

"We only seek partial cancellation. The agreement to ship the merchandise may stand, but the price provisions should be modified. The defendant is entitled to amend the counterclaim. The Supreme Court has held that the provisions of law respecting amendments must be given the most generous interpretation."

"Mr. Bochatz," I responded, "you have exhausted both my patience and my generosity. The motion is dismissed. Any further comment?"

"No, my lord. It is true that you have been patient. Despite everything that has happened in this courtroom, I still ask that the action be dismissed."

I glanced at the clock and intoned, "The plaintiff has proven the essential allegations of its claim. The defendant failed to prove its counterclaim. The defendant is condemned to pay the plaintiff the sum of $249,000, with interest and costs. The Court is adjourned."

Linda instructed everyone to rise.

As he left the courtroom, Albert Morrison's voice called from the background.

"Your Honour, Your Honour, you forgot your box of Kleenex."

9

All in the Family

The most emotionally draining experience for a judge is to spend a month in the family division. The general principles of the Divorce Act are rapidly mastered, but the application of these principles to myriad individual situations requires insight, patience, and a dash of good luck. A touch of good-natured humour can preserve judicial equilibrium, even if the chuckle must be postponed until the court adjourns. In family court, more than anywhere else, the judge learns the limitations of the law and the boundaries of his authority.

The successful resolution of a dispute is not always possible. Financial resources may not be sufficient to assure both parties of an adequate standard of living. Neither parent may be fit to care for the children. Can one order the payment of a sum beyond the means of the party? How does one compel an unwilling ten-year-old child to see a parent? How can children spend Christmas with different parents in different cities simultaneously?

Some contested divorces and custody and alimony hearings become charged with tension and the contest descends

133

to the nadir of brutality. Others rapidly assume the theatrical character of comedy and even farce. Throughout, the judge must remain distant in a dispute where the litigants frequently seek to play on his sympathy and involve him personally. In the family division, the unexpected, the unusual, and even the absurd are commonplace. Variety is the daily routine.

One quiet day, my regularly scheduled assignments were completed before noon. The clerk informed the office of the Master of the Rolls (who distributes cases among the judges) that I would be available that afternoon for other cases. It had been a slow day throughout the palace, and I was asked to hear three uncontested divorces. It appeared that the afternoon would be uneventful as well.

The session opened and the first case was called. I began to flip through the file nonchalantly. The silence that usually precedes the hearing of a case was broken by an attractive, dark-haired woman, who was addressing me.

"I am the defendant in this case and I have decided to represent myself. My lawyer will not be here. Something terrible is happening and you must prevent a great and further injustice."

"One moment, please. Since you are the defendant, I must first ask the plaintiff's lawyer to introduce himself. The plaintiff makes his proof first and then you will be allowed all the time necessary to offer proof and to present your arguments."

"But he will ask you to pronounce a divorce. And that is not what the law requires. You must not hear these things. My husband and I are still in love with each other and they have prevented us from seeing each other. I must see him."

"Did you not have a chance to see each other in the corridor before the opening of the Court?" I asked.

"No, I have always been prevented from seeing him.

Please, let me read you the sections of the Divorce Act that say what you must attempt to bring about a reconciliation."

"I am aware of those sections of the law and my obligations. I am also obliged to permit your husband to present his evidence and arguments. As plaintiff, he is entitled to proceed first."

"Oh please, *Monsieur le juge*. Do something to prevent this great tragedy. No one will listen to me."

I turned to the husband's attorney. "Mr. Johnson, can you enlighten the Court as to what is transpiring in this file?"

"Well, my lord. This couple has been separated for . . . "

"We have not been separated," interjected the defendant. "They kept us apart. No one will allow me to see my husband. He loves me. I know he does. If only I can see him for five minutes, everything will be resolved. Please, *Monsieur le juge!*"

"Mr. Johnson, do you have any objection to my calling a fifteen-minute recess, during which time the defendant can speak to her husband in the corridor?"

Johnson turned towards his client. They exchanged a whispered comment. He then looked up and replied, "No, my lord. We will consent and my client will speak to his wife in the adjoining cubicle."

"Thank you. Mrs. Bédard, I will adjourn for a few minutes so that you can talk to your husband. When the Court resumes, I must allow your husband to present his evidence and arguments, just as I must permit you to offer your evidence. Is that understood?"

"Yes, thank you."

I glanced at my usher and announced, "The Court will adjourn until a quarter to three."

Fifteen minutes later when court reconvened, I asked the defendant, "Mrs. Bédard, did you have an opportunity to speak to your husband?"

"Yes, but he is under some sort of spell. I know he still loves me but he will not say so."

"Madam, I must now ask you to sit down and allow your husband's attorney to proceed. You may question each witness after your husband's attorney has done so."

Bruce Johnson called the plaintiff as his first witness. He explained that he and his wife had been separated for seven years and that for the last five years he had been living with another woman, whom he wished to marry. He had not seen his wife for five years, but received frequent letters and phone calls from her. Despite several moves and an unlisted phone number, his wife always managed to find his new address and number.

When Bruce Johnson had finished questioning his client, I turned to the defendant.

"You may now cross-examine — that is, question — the witness."

"Why did you leave me?" she asked. "Don't you know that I love you and will never let you go?"

"I know," mumbled the plaintiff.

"Why, why, why do you let them keep us apart?" she asked, as she burst into tears.

Mr. Bédard remained silent, shifting his weight from side to side. His complexion turned white, and then even whiter as his wife's sobs filled the courtroom.

"The Court will adjourn for five minutes," I announced. My usher had already opened the door in anticipation.

When we reconvened, Bruce Johnson announced that he had no further evidence to offer. However, his client's companion was available for questioning if I so desired. I declined the offer.

I then turned to Mrs. Bédard and asked, "Do you wish to present any evidence?"

"No, it will not do any good. You believe my husband. You are working with them. Please . . . do not issue a divorce. My husband still loves me. It is your duty to make a reconciliation. I will read you what the Divorce Act says. Please!"

"Is there any further evidence to be offered?"

"No," replied Mr. Johnson.

"Mrs. Bédard?"

She sobbed aloud and did not respond.

I proceeded to pronounce the divorce. Mrs. Bédard sobbed throughout. Mr. Bédard looked even whiter, if possible, and Bruce Johnson stared off into space.

When I had completed intoning the prescribed formula, my usher walked over to help the sobbing defendant. Mr. Bédard and his attorney remained seated, impassive.

I announced, "The Court will adjourn for fifteen minutes."

Before I could rise, an attorney rushed up to the bench and said, "Please, my lord, please do not adjourn now. My client is next on the roll and this is a case of extreme urgency. Please hear us before the adjournment."

"Mr. Lambert," I said, "I noticed you were sitting in the courtroom during the past hour. You can appreciate that these hearings are not always easy and I feel that an adjournment is necessary for me and the court officers to recover our composure. Besides, I have noted that your client has been married for some time, and fail to see why an additional fifteen minutes of married life will harm her."

"My lord," he implored, "this is a real emergency. Please look at my client."

For the first time, I noticed the heavy-set woman who had been seated at his side. "My client is pregnant. The father of the child is a man other than her husband, and the labour pains have begun."

As I looked again at the woman, she caught her breath, sighed gently, and smiled at me. This was immediately followed by a much deeper sigh as she clutched her stomach.

"Mr. Lambert, proceed immediately and quickly."

I do not know who holds the world's record for the fastest divorce hearing, but if I did not set the record then and there, I at least earned an honourable mention. Within approximately three minutes, the hearing was completed and the judgment pronounced.

"Stay with them until they have left the building," I instructed my usher, as I rose. "The Court will adjourn. Good luck, Madam, I wish you an easy delivery. The Court will adjourn."

Contrary to usual practice, I opened the door myself and walked quickly to my office. The quiet afternoon had been transformed. What would happen next? Trouble always comes in threes.

Twenty minutes later, after having a slow cup of coffee and after being informed by my usher that the pregnant plaintiff had left the building safely and still pregnant, I returned to the courtroom.

The next file looked routine. It was a request for a divorce on the grounds that the parties had been living apart for more than three years. The wife was not present in the courtroom. Her attorney explained.

"My lord, my client is not present today, for reasons which will be explained shortly. She does not contest the granting of the divorce. In fact, she requests that the divorce be granted today and that you declare the divorce to have immediate effect and waive the ninety-day waiting period. If the Court permits, my colleague, Ms. Warden, who is a member of the Bar of British Columbia, is here today, and with the Court's permission, will make special representations in that respect."

A woman sitting in the audience wearing a smartly styled tweed suit, rose and said, "Yes, Your Lordship, may I address the Court?"

"I shall be pleased to hear you," I responded, "but first I should like to hear the proof respecting the divorce. If it is sufficient, I shall render the judgment of divorce and then hear any special applications to shorten or eliminate the waiting period until the divorce takes effect. In the meantime, you may sit beside Montreal counsel for the defendant."

The proof of the grounds for divorce was made and I rendered the divorce. I then looked up and said, "The Court will now entertain further motions."

Ms. Warden stood and addressed me.

"Your Lordship, thank you for your consideration in permitting me to address the Court. The defendant in this case is a resident of the city of Vancouver and a client of our office. For the past number of years she has been living with a gentleman who is a client of our office as well. I am personally aware of the facts I now tell you, and I am prepared to be sworn and testify to their correctness."

"That will not be necessary. I accept your representations as true, being made under your oath of office."

"Well," she continued, "the gentleman with whom the defendant has been living has cancer. The doctors at the hospital where he is being treated inform us that he has only a few days left. He wishes to marry the defendant before he dies, and obviously can do so only if the final divorce decree is rendered today. I am in Montreal for the day and have reservations to fly back to Vancouver on the seven o'clock flight."

I turned to the plaintiff's attorney.

"Do you have any representations to make with respect to this application?"

"No, my lord."

"Considering that it is in the public interest and considering the representations of counsel, the application is granted. I do not know if you are aware of the system of registration of judgments. The judgment must be transcribed, registered in the office on the main floor, and certified by an official of the Court. I don't know if you can complete all of this today. I shall help. Come to my office in ten minutes."

As the Court adjourned, I instructed the clerk to bring the file to my office. I called my secretary from the corridor phone and told her to contact the office on the main floor and advise them I would send a judgment down shortly and ordered them to remain open until it was received and registered. After I returned to my office, my secretary typed both the judgment of divorce and the judgment eliminating the delay after which it was to take effect. I signed both judgments and she brought them downstairs to be registered and certified. When the attorneys arrived in my office, I invited them to have a coffee while we waited together for my secretary to return. At a quarter to five I handed Ms. Warden the certified copies of the judgments.

Two weeks later I received a letter from Vancouver informing me that the attorney had made her plane. The defendant and her friend had married in the hospital room. He had died three days later.

Justice B. J. Greenberg is undoubtedly one of the most brilliant and able jurists in this country. He strives to project the image of the model judge in both his public and his private life. He is the epitome of impartiality, objectivity, and restraint, and shuns unseemly displays of emotion.

Few people are aware that his Achilles heel is a small, hairy, ribboned, yappy Yorkie whom he drags behind him on a shoelace like an après-ski boot. Twice daily he strolls proudly around the block displaying his prized dog to neighbours and admirers, and the dog is a novelty, since Yorkies are relatively rare in this country. In France, however, the breed abounds, and when Justice Greenberg attended a judicial seminar in Strasbourg, France, he roamed the streets in search of Yorkies so he could engage their masters in conversation and compare their exploits and characteristics with those of his pet.

One day Justice Greenberg was presiding in family court. The parties were engaged in a custody dispute and each sought to influence the judge by describing the ideal home environment they had created for the children. The husband's testimony strained the judge's impartiality and demeanour.

"Could you describe the house where you propose to receive your children?"

"It's a large, detached, single family home with all the amenities."

"Is there a separate bedroom for each child?"

"Yes."

"Do you have any animals in the house?"

"Yes, I have a blond retriever who is friendly and gentle. The children love to sit on his back and play with him."

"Doesn't your wife also have a dog?"

"No, she has a Yorkie."

"But a Yorkie is a dog."

"No, it isn't! A Yorkie is not a dog. It's a weasel!"

To this day, Justice Greenberg steadfastly denies that the exchange had any impact on his decision to award custody to the mother.

Shortly after his appointment to the Bench, Justice Lagacé was assigned to the family division. Upon entering the courtroom he observed armed guards in each corner. In response to his whispered question, the usher explained that he was to have the distinct privilege of presiding at the divorce hearing of Jean Laverdure, Public Enemy no. 2, who was being brought from a high-security penitentiary for the hearing.

When Laverdure's name was called, the door opened and the plaintiff entered with hands and feet chained, flanked by four armed guards. While this transpired, a slight, dark-haired spectator in the rear of the courtroom rose and began to speak, but he was rapidly silenced by the usher.

Unaccustomed to scenes of this type, Justice Lagacé asked the police officers if they would unshackle the plaintiff. The officer in charge responded that Laverdure had a history of prison escapes, including two escapes from courtrooms. He remained shackled when the court clerk politely requested the prisoner to state his name and address. The unexpected reply was: "None of your business."

The witness cooperated and responded more politely after the judge repeated the question. At this point, the spectator who had previously tried to speak rose once more, and again, he was silenced by the usher.

Mr. Justice Lagacé, who felt that he had more than he needed in activity, glared at the spectator and threatened to have him removed if there were further interruptions.

The plaintiff's attorney began his questioning. "Were you married to Marie Laverdure?"

The witness responded, "*Non.*"

The courtroom silence was interrupted by the noise of the same spectator rising and exclaiming, "*Monsieur le juge . . .*"

The judge glared but the man continued, "*Monsieur le juge,* he is not Jean Laverdure, I am Jean Laverdure. He was not married to Marie Laverdure. I was married to Marie Laverdure. He is not asking for a divorce. I am asking for a divorce."

A few further questions elicited the information that the spectator had also been a prisoner in the same penitentiary as the chained Public Enemy no. 2, and had been released on parole several days earlier. The police had made a simple error of mistaken identity between the two men who happened to bear the same name.

Public Enemy no. 2 was turned about and marched out of the courtroom with his police escort. The real plaintiff was divorced a few moments later.

Under the old Divorce Act, the judgment was a double proceeding. The judge heard the case and rendered a *decree nisi* — that is, a preliminary, conditional judgment. After the lapse of ninety days, one of the parties could present a further application to the Court for a *decree absolute*, or final judgment of divorce. Usually the application was presented a few days after the expiration of the ninety-day waiting period.

In one case before me, the *decree nisi* had been pronounced five years prior to the application for final judgment. Understandably, I was curious about this excessive delay. The husband testified that during this period he had had no contact with his wife other than once when he returned to the family residence for a stay of a few days. He denied having shared his wife's bed during this time.

When the wife testified, she explained that after the preliminary judgment, she and her husband had been reconciled. The husband had continued to work in the business she owned, and she produced sixty-five salary cheques in support of this contention. She testified that the husband had moved back into the family residence, and they had lived and slept together as husband and wife throughout the five years.

I was perplexed by their dramatically different versions of events. True, a witness may forget a distant event or detail, but can a man forget five years of sexual relationship?

The truth became evident when I heard the corroborating testimony of the neighbour downstairs. He confirmed that he had seen the husband around the family residence continually, and specifically remembered the nightly slamming of the garage door and the heavy footsteps as he mounted the stairs to the flat. Unable to remain silent in the face of the husband's obviously untrue evidence, I glared at him from the bench and asked, "Did you testify that you had no relations with your wife during the past five years?"

His disconcerted attorney whispered aloud, "The judge remembers what you said!"

I reluctantly maintained the husband's application after the wife conceded that there was no longer any chance of reconciliation and the contestation was really an attempt to punish him for the failed reconciliation.

143

Parties and even attorneys can become so caught up in a case that they overlook a simple solution. The trial of *Chavez* versus *Martineau* illustrates this situation.

Ms. Martineau and Mr. Chavez had a brief but torrid romance. A child was born of their relationship. They separated without marrying. Ms. Martineau correctly felt that her former lover should pay one-half of the cost of the child's upbringing. She sued successfully and obtained a judgment declaring Mr. Chavez the child's father and obliging him to pay child support.

Mr. Chavez then counter-sued. He had discovered that the child was registered as Joseph-Louis Henry Martineau. As the father, he now requested that the name be changed to Joseph-Louis Henry Chavez-Martineau. The procedures were bitterly contested. When the parties first appeared in court, the judge asked if an attorney represented the interests of the child. When the question went unanswered, he appointed an attorney for the child and postponed the case to a later date when he would not be available. The case was fixed before me.

When I entered the courtroom, three lawyers introduced themselves: one for each of the parties and one for the child. Ms. Martineau's lawyer immediately presented a motion for the dismissal of the proceedings on the grounds that the procedure was wrongly taken and that I lacked jurisdiction. Mr. Chavez's attorney responded that he had numerous authorities to the contrary. A mock epic battle was brewing.

I quietly asked the attorney for the child, "Does the child have any particular interest in whether the family is Martineau or Chavez-Martineau?"

"No," she responded. "The child has not reached school age and there are no records or other documents that would require change other than the birth certificate."

At this point, I looked at the parties and their attorneys and said, "I have a suggestion. Mind you, I have not heard your arguments and am not prejudging. Surely the person who should decide this matter is the child. His family name is the subject of this suit.

"May I suggest that the conclusions of the proceedings be changed to delete the hyphen? The parties could then consent to the application, and the child's name would be changed to Joseph Louis Henry Chavez Martineau. When the child is eighteen he will have the option of calling himself 'Martineau' or 'Chavez Martineau'." After hasty consultation between the parties and their counsel, everyone agreed. The application was granted by consent. I never did find out if I had jurisdiction.

Chutzpah has been described as "not nerve and not gall, but the fine flowering of the two." Nowhere is this quality more apparent than in family court. One applicant had beaten his wife so badly that she was hospitalized and suffered three broken ribs. The police investigated and laid criminal charges of assault, whereupon the accused presented an application for reduction of his child and spousal support obligations on the grounds that he must conserve his funds to pay the cost of defending himself in the criminal courts.

Emergencies arise daily in family court and some problems cannot be postponed for a month or two until a judge is available to hear witnesses and arguments. The typical emergency concerns manifestations of violence towards consorts and children; acute lack of money to purchase necessities; obstruction and denial of visiting rights; and anticipated flight by one of the parties and the children from the country. Each day, one judge is assigned to deal with the most urgent of these cases. The judge makes interim orders on the basis of affidavits and brief arguments. These orders are legal patches which remain in effect until the matter can be heard in the normal manner; they are subject to revision and correction by the judge who hears the parties a month or two later. Verbal applications are common. Heightened feverish activity is the rule. The continuous movement of people in and out of the courtroom contrasts sharply with the sombre atmosphere in other courtrooms. Confusion and surprise are inevitable, intuition and judicial ingenuity, common sense, and rapid decisions are prerequisites.

Lawyer Linda Robinson once interrupted the proceedings to inform me that her client, the plaintiff, was being subjected to unfair harassment in the corridor of the courthouse, where the defendant was exhibiting a nude photograph of her. I ordered the clerk to call that case next. The parties had never married, but had lived together for eight months. A child had been born of their relationship and the father was seeking visiting rights. The mother was terrified by the child's father and wanted an order prohibiting all contact with her, the child, and her family. There was an assault charge pending before the criminal courts.

"Before I get into the merits of these applications, I wish to clear up the matter of the photographs," I announced.

"Your Lordship," said Robinson, "I have subpoenaed Officer Demers of the Police Department as a witness. He was in the hall when the incident occurred and can explain what happened."

"Fine, go ahead."

Officer Demers testified that he had been standing in the corridor and had seen the incident. He saw the defendant approach the plaintiff. The defendant had a broad leer on his face and was carrying a brown envelope. The plaintiff had shouted and people had looked up. The officer had rushed over to see what had caused the commotion but had not seen any pictures.

"Ms. Robinson," I asked, "do you want me to hear any further testimony respecting this incident in the corridor?"

"Yes," she replied, "Mr. Peter Gordon, the defendant."

After the defendant was sworn in, Robinson asked, "Mr.

Gordon, did you exhibit any pictures of the plaintiff in the corridor of the courthouse today?"

"No," he answered.

"Do you realize you are under oath?"

"Yes."

There was a silence in the room. I decided to ask a few questions personally.

"Mr. Gordon, did you bring any pictures of the plaintiff to Court with you today?"

"Yes."

"Are these pictures in any place where you can get them in the next five minutes?"

"Yes, they are in my briefcase."

"Is any part of the plaintiff's body not covered in the pictures?"

"Yes."

"Would it be fair to say that she is totally or partially nude in any of the pictures?"

"Yes."

"Is it possible that someone in the corridor caught a glimpse of one or more of these photographs at any time this morning?"

"Well, I had the envelope with me, it dropped on the floor, and one picture might have fallen out for an instant."

"Why did you bring these pictures to court today?"

"To give them to Miss . . . the plaintiff."

"Please do so. NOW!"

Peter Gordon walked over to the plaintiff and handed her a brown envelope. The incident was closed.

Joseph and Leah Gaon had been married in Morocco in the early 1950s. Shortly afterwards, they emigrated to Montreal. Leah adapted to the customs, lifestyles, and commercial realities of her new country. She passed the civil service exams and got a full-time job with the government. Throughout the years of marriage, she worked steadily, with only brief inter-ruptions when her children were born. In addition to the income from her regular employment, she earned extra money by baking Moroccan-style cakes for a local bakery, baby-sitting neighbour's children, and keeping a watchful eye on homes in her vicinity when their occupants were away on holidays.

Joseph failed to adapt to life in Canada. He pursued the big deal and the fast buck, but both eluded him. His plans and ideas were overambitious and his business ventures un-derfunded. He earned the occasional few dollars by obliging some of the wheeler-dealers he idolized and whose company he sought. Although virtually unemployed, he did manage to earn spending money and was content to leave the support of the family and management of the household to his wife.

Four years after arriving in Canada, Leah and Joseph purchased a duplex in St. Laurent. The down payment was minimal and was paid out of their joint account. The home was registered in Joseph's name, although he had not made any deposits in the joint account. Leah budgeted her re-sources to make sure that the mortgage instalments were paid punctually. She would bring her first pay cheque of the month to the accountant in the bank and wait to see the deposit recorded and the mortgage payment deducted from the joint account. She adopted this precaution after Joseph once man-aged to withdraw funds from the account for one of his "deals" before the payment for the monthly mortgage instal-ment had been cleared.

The years passed, the children grew older, and Leah's income grew steadily. By careful budgeting of the household expenses, she managed to pay the mortgage on the duplex and put aside extra money. The family enjoyed a modest but solid status within the community of new Canadians of Moroccan descent.

In 1978, when house prices declined, Leah seized the

opportunity to upgrade the family's living conditions. She purchased a bungalow in a better neighbourhood, and the family moved. The duplex was rented to provide revenue and re-mortgaged to obtain funds for the down payment on the bungalow. This time the house was registered in the names of both Leah and Joseph.

Life in the new home was more pleasant than in the old one. The children had grown into confident teenagers who attended university. They were now closer to the campus and Leah could expect them to bring home a better class of friends. These were important considerations as the children approached marriageable age. Leah continued working in the public service and her baked goods became more popular. On weekends, she now operated a small catering business for private parties.

Around this time, Joseph began to despair of ever finding the big deal and began to drink heavily. His despondency fed on itself and his consumption of alcohol increased. One night in 1983, while wandering around downtown in an inebriated state, he was struck by a car and seriously injured. He was brought to the Montreal General Hospital, where he stayed for months on end. For a while he was totally paralyzed. Gradually, with medical care and multiple operations, part of his strength returned, but he never recovered full strength in his lower arms. He could write slowly but could not do any strenuous physical labour.

Though exhausted by her work and matrimonial responsibilities, Leah spent many hours visiting her husband in the hospital. But during his period of convalescence, she became aware for the first time that she was self-sufficient. When her husband returned home, she would no longer respond to his every request. She saw that he lacked the strength upon which she had thought herself dependent. Self-sufficiency turned to independence, and her love for Joseph, which had waned and turned into indifference, was now transformed into disdain. Six months after Joseph's release from hospital, Leah decided to sue for divorce. The decision was difficult. She was racked by guilt for abandoning her husband at the moment of his vulnerability and breaking from a religious and family tradition of dependence, but she could no longer endure the prospect of sharing his bed.

Joseph viewed the procedures as a liberation and an opportunity. His attorneys investigated the laws governing the division of family property, and after consultation with the Moroccan Consulate and certain rabbinic authorities, they advised him that he should claim all of the family's assets. Because he had lived in Morocco at the time of his marriage, Moroccan law governed the distribution of the family assets, and that law provided that when persons of the Jewish faith married and executed a contract known as a *Ketubah*, in accordance with the requirements of ancient Jewish Talmudic law, that law would govern their matrimonial regime and determine their respective rights to family property upon divorce. In Talmudic law, women did not enjoy full civil and property rights. The family was a unit and its assets were under the control of, and ultimately were the property of, the husband.

The trial began with the usual litany of complaints and reproaches. I was rapidly convinced that the parties would never be reconciled and that divorce was inevitable. I informed both attorneys that I was satisfied as to the grounds for the divorce and would hear the evidence respecting alimony and distribution of family assets.

Joseph had attempted to obtain the sympathy of the court by emphasizing his weakened physical condition. His neurologist testified that he would never have sufficient strength in his arms to drive an automobile safely, that he could not even sign his name, and that it would take many months and perhaps years before he would be able to drink a glass of wine without shaking and spilling the contents.

This evidence proved untrustworthy. During the first break, I instructed my usher to place a glass of water on the table in front of the witness box. Two or three times that morning, I saw Joseph reach out, lift the glass, and sip the water slowly. The assertion that he would be unable to write or sign his name was contradicted by the existence of his sworn affidavits in the court record. Either the affidavits were forgeries or Joseph could, in fact, sign his name. When he finally testified, I casually asked him if in fact he had executed these documents, and he replied positively. I did not ask about his capacity to drive an automobile. However, one morning when he was late for court, he volunteered the information that he had driven to the courthouse and had had difficulty parking.

The Court in Quebec is officially unaware of the content of foreign law. Until the contrary is proven, the Court must assume that the foreign law is identical to Quebec law. To establish that the foreign law *is* different, judges, and other experts are called as witnesses. According to this requirement, Joseph would have to prove to my satisfaction the content of the Moroccan and Talmudic law if he wanted his case to be decided in accordance with their dispositions.

Part of this proof was simple. His attorney had filed a letter from the Moroccan consul confirming that under the terms of Moroccan law as it existed in 1952, persons of the Jewish faith who executed a *Ketubah* prior to their marriage were governed by its terms and by the Talmudic law. The content of the letter was not contested, but I asked the attorneys if the original *Ketubah* and a translation could be filed. The court record contained a summary of the document. They informed me that the original was in the possession of an expert witness who would testify later.

The first witness was a law professor, Keith Townsend. Joseph's lawyer asked him his qualifications as an expert and he responded at length about his experience and writings.

None of these appeared particularly relevant because he did not mention having written, studied, or read any material, or having had any particular experience in the field of either Moroccan or Jewish Talmudic law.

Joseph's lawyer looked up and asked, "Will the Court accept Professor Townsend as an expert witness?"

I glanced in the direction of Leah's counsel. He was impassive. Doubts gnawed at me. I looked at Professor Townsend.

"Professor, are you by any chance a member of the Bar of Morocco?"

"No," he replied.

"Are you an ordained rabbi?"

"No, my lord," he answered with a smile.

"Do you speak Aramaic?" I asked.

"No."

"In what language is this *Ketubah* drafted?"

"Aramaic."

"The Court rejects Professor Townsend as an expert witness on Jewish law and *Ketubot*."

I subsequently learned from a colleague of Dr. Townsend that he had been engaged to testify as an expert witness a few days before the trial and that he knew nothing about the subject and had canvassed his Jewish colleagues' opinions on the subject during the previous day. On the morning of the trial, he had boasted about the testimony he would give and was embarrassed to return to the faculty at ten-thirty that morning and confess that the Court would not accept him as an expert. An old friend of his who teaches at the same university commented, "The judge was right!"

The next witness had impressive qualifications and an imposing appearance, which was enhanced by his white beard and reddish complexion. He was a graduate of the University of Strasbourg, where he had taught for several years and had been a judge in a Jewish Religious Tribunal in Morocco during the fifties before he emigrated to Canada. He was now retired and devoted himself to writing and doing the occasional guest lecture. He was questioned by Joseph's counsel.

"Professor, did you have occasion to study the Talmudic law respecting divorces?"

"Yes, I studied at religious schools and many times reviewed and re-read the volumes of *Kedushin* and *Gittin* in the Talmud."

"Did you, as a judge in the Jewish religious court in Morocco, have occasion to apply this law?"

"Yes, I did."

"Professor, have you read the *Ketubah* signed by Joseph and Leah Gaon?"

"I did. The original *Ketubah* was brought to my office. I have a translation of its important details with me. As you can see, I have only translated the details of the marriage and the proper names of the parties, because the other information does not change from one *Ketubah* to the next. These terms were prescribed by the rabbis of the Talmud and have not changed."

"Sir," I interjected, "in what language is the *Ketubah* drafted?"

"Aramic."

"Do you read and understand Aramic?"

"Of course, Your Lordship. The Talmud is written in Aramic as are all *Ketubot*," he replied.

"Thank you, continue."

"Professor, what is the answer to the following question? Under the Talmudic law, as established by the rabbis of the Talmud and as applied by you and other judges in the Rabbinic Courts of Morocco in the 1950's, if a Jewish couple executed a *Ketubah*, married, and was subsequently divorced, how is the family property to be divided between the spouses?"

"The matter is described in the *Ketubah*. The wife is

entitled to receive two hundred *zekukim* (measures) of silver. That sum can be translated into Moroccan currency . . . it would equal . . . let me think . . . 14,000 Canadian dollars. Yes, the wife is entitled to receive $14,000. All other property is the exclusive property of the husband."

The attorney sat down slowly. "No further questions." Joseph smiled and I announced, "The Court will adjourn for fifteen minutes."

Following the recess, I asked, "Will you file the original *Ketubah* and a certified English or French translation in the court record?"

"Yes, my lord, the documents will be filed tomorrow."

I turned to Leah's attorney, "Cross-examination?"

"No questions."

For less than a minute I reflected upon whether it would be appropriate for me to ask a question or two and then proceeded.

"Professor, you have explained the Talmudic rules which govern the division of matrimonial property following the granting of a divorce to a couple married in Morocco after executing a *Ketubah*."

"Yes."

"Would you now explain to me, what are the obligations of a husband under the *Ketubah* and Talmud during the marriage? In other words, move back from the divorce and tell me about the role of the husband and wife under Jewish Talmudic law during the marriage."

"*Monsieur le juge*, the Talmud provides that every husband who executes a *Ketubah* and marries must assume the obligation to provide for his wife's needs as befits a daughter of Israel. He must provide her with a house — that is, shelter, clothing, food, and all other reasonable requirements."

"Under the law of the Talmud and the *Ketubah*, what would be the consequences if the husband should fail to respect these obligations?"

The professor looked up pensively, stoked his beard, and replied, "Where the husband fails to provide his wife with shelter, clothing and food as befits a daughter of Israel, the wife is permitted to work and keep the fruits or product of her work."

At this point, Joseph's attorney rose and said, "My lord, I see that it is now four-thirty and I had promised the professor that we would adjourn at that hour as he is guest lecturer in Talmudic studies at the Seminary."

"The Court is adjourned until nine-thirty tomorrow, when the testimony of the professor will resume and the *Ketubah* will be filed."

When court resumed the following day, the professor was not present. I looked up and asked, "Will the professor be here soon? Have you located the original *Ketubah*?"

Joseph's counsel responded, "Your Lordship, the professor has informed me that he is unable to locate the original *Ketubah*. In addition, he must conduct a very important class today and cannot attend." Turning towards Leah's attorney, he continued, "My colleague and I have agreed that since the *Ketubah* cannot be found, we will ask you to assume that the Moroccan law and Talmudic law are identical to Quebec law and decide this case in accordance with the Civil Code of Quebec."

I glanced in the direction of Leah's attorney, who nodded agreement. "So be it. Proceed."

When the hearing was concluded, I rendered judgment. The majority of the assets were awarded to Leah. She was ordered to pay a minimal allowance to her husband for the following two years to help him until he was fully recovered from his accident. Joseph's appeal against my judgment was dismissed the following year.

Leah's lawyer has since lectured in both Canada and the United States about this case he won!

In another dispute respecting ownership of the family residence, the husband claimed that he had purchased the home with personal savings and the proceeds of a gift from his father in the amount of $25,000. The father was summoned as a witness to corroborate the husband's testimony. The introductory question yielded an unexpected response.

"Sir, what is your relationship with the plaintiff?"

"Very good!" replied the father.

The father's testimony was particularly effective. In a simple, straightforward manner he provided details of the various gifts he had made to his son over a five-year period.

Although the husband's attorney had proven the point, he considered it prudent to call the family accountant to provide additional information from the tax returns filed. He had obviously prepared for his day in court. When asked to take the oath, however, the accountant glanced at the Bible, then looked up at me and asked, "Is this a Jewish Bible or a Christian Bible?"

"If you examine the volume before you, you will find that both the Old Testament and the New Testament have been bound in one volume. I invite you to turn to the Testament of your choice and take the oath," I answered.

"I wouldn't know the difference."

"Well, if you don't know the difference, you should not have asked the question," commented the wife's attorney who must have read my mind. After this unfortunate opening gambit, the accountant's testimony lost much of its impact.

Just before the afternoon session, I was informed that the wife's attorney had lost his briefcase. I waited in my office until three o'clock when it was finally found. Then, fifteen minutes after the session began, the lawyer asked for another adjournment because of difficulties with his briefcase.

"But I understand that you have found the lost briefcase," I commented.

"Yes, my lord," he said, "but it's locked and I don't have the combination."

I granted the adjournment. When we resumed half an hour

later, it was the wife's turn to interrupt the proceedings. "I have to catch a plane to Arizona tonight," she said. "Please instruct the lawyers to ask me only the important questions."

Fortunately, her testimony was concluded in time for her to leave, and the rest of the trial was completed in her absence. Because she had a medical condition that made her unable to endure Canada's cold winters, the wife spent six months each year in Arizona. She had launched the lawsuit because she wanted the family residence for security and suggested that her husband and the children move in with his parents. It was little wonder that she lost the case.

Two weeks later, I received a call about the case at my office.

"Judge Steinberg?"

"Yes, speaking."

"You don't know me, but I know you."

"Yes, what can I do for you?"

"Oh, did you make a mistake in the case of my friend, Sandra!"

"I'm sorry. I do not understand who you are or why you are calling."

"Judge Steinberg, my friend Sandra does not know how to explain a case. If you knew what I know, you would not have decided what you did."

"Madam, I am a judge. I only know the facts I hear in court."

"Really?"

"Yes, madam."

"And you didn't even give her half the house. Isn't there a law that you should give the wife half the house?"

"No, not that I am aware of."

"Well, there should be such a law. You're a judge. You should tell the government to make such a law."

"Madam, where do you live?"

"Côte St. Luc."

"Madam, your member of the provincial legislature happens to be the Minister of Justice. I suggest you call him and ask him to propose such a law. Thank you."

I do not know if she ever called the Minister of Justice, but several months later, the government did introduce a law requiring the equal division between divorcing parties of the value of family residences, furniture, automobiles, and pension plans acquired during the marriage.

10

The Assizes

On June 15, 1215, the Barons of England confronted King John at Runnymede and started the negotiations that resulted in the signing of the great Charter, Magna Carta. "No free man," they proclaimed, "shall be arrested or imprisoned or deprived of his freehold or outlawed or banished or in any way ruined, nor will we take or order action against him, except by the lawful judgment of his equals and according to the law of the land. To no one will we sell, to no one will we refuse or delay right or justice."

The rule of law was now enshrined in a document signed by the King and the arbitrary exercise of government authority was prohibited. There would be no punishment or confiscation unless a crime was committed and the guilt of the accused under law was established before a judge or jury. When a person was detained without cause, a writ of Habeas Corpus could order that the detained person be brought before a judge so that the legality of the detention be adjudged. Those who were unjustly detained would be released.

The Magna Carta was the product of a primitive feudal

society, and initially, it did not spawn the institutions needed to create an environment where freedom would flourish and law could rule. In the ensuing centuries, it was restricted in application, frequently misunderstood, and often ignored. Yet for almost eight hundred years, the principles of the Magna Carta were taken seriously and expanded. Virtually all subsequent constitutional, civil, and human rights legislation, declarations of independence, bills of rights, and charters of rights in the English-speaking world reinforced these principles. The long, tortuous path through history led from the fields of Runnymede to the door of the courtroom where I was assigned to welcome a panel of several hundred prospective jurors.

I had been warned by experienced colleagues that the atmosphere would resemble that of a championship prize fight. Hundreds of people selected at random from the electoral lists are summoned. They crowd into a courtroom designed to hold fewer than one hundred spectators. Jury candidates stand in the rear, sit in the jury box, crowd the aisles, and occupy every other available spot. Most are apprehensive, some are reluctant, and several are outraged that they have been removed from the stream of daily life and may be required to spend days, weeks, or even months on an unsought assignment in forbidding premises. Each prospective juror has heard or read of a trial that lasted for months, fears some form of reprisal, and would rather watch *L.A. Law* than get in on the action in real life.

Inevitably, the entry of the judge is delayed because the court clerk has not completed the roll call, people have wandered into the wrong floor, or the courtroom is overcrowded. To top things off, the air conditioning and ventilation are almost always inadequate. As the judge sweeps into the room to the sound of "All rise," he can sense the tension and curiosity.

The judge's welcoming remarks include an expression of

appreciation to the audience, a brief comment on the history and importance of the jury system, reassurance that the forthcoming case will not take ten months, public admonition of those who failed to respond to the subpoena, and an invitation to those who seek exemption to remain following adjournment to be received individually by the judge.

I managed to feign confidence and acquitted myself well during the opening speech, but I was totally unprepared for the hearing on exemptions. Only wit and humour saved the day.

The first applicant entered the room where I was seated, the Crown attorney on my right and the court clerk on my left. As I looked up inquisitively, he asked, "Your Honour, do you accept Newfies on your jury?"

"Are you, sir, a native of the Province of Newfoundland?" I asked.

"No," he replied, "I was born in New Brunswick but we Maritimers are all the same." I waved him out and he turned and left. The next two people requested exemption on medical grounds: one was slated for surgery; the other was unable to remain in a seated position for a prolonged period because of lower back problems. These were the easy ones.

A gentleman entered carrying a white cane, accompanied by a Seeing Eye dog. "I presume you request an exemption because of your blindness?"

"Oh no," he replied, "I came to tell you that I wish to serve on a jury."

The purpose of the jury system is to ensure just treatment of the accused. Juries are not balanced as to sex, colour or religion and cannot accomodate persons who suffer from an infirmity that impedes their ability to observe, hear, and weigh the evidence. This man could not form part of a jury. How could I let him down lightly?

"Does your dog accompany you on all occasions?" I asked.

"Yes, I cannot manage without him," he responded.

"Unfortunately, the deliberation rooms are small, and I am concerned that if you are chosen, other members of the jury may feel uncomfortable in confined quarters with your dog during the period of deliberations."

"I guess you are right," he observed. "Thank you for your consideration."

"Exemption granted," I said with relief and shook his hand as he turned to leave.

Juror 79 informed me that he was an insurance agent operating a one-man business and would be deprived of his livelihood if obliged to serve. I granted his request. Juror 136 told me that he directed a business with over 729 employees and could not possibly take off the time to serve on the jury. After asking him how many weeks of holiday he had taken the previous year, I informed him that the other 728 people would have to cover for him. The request for exemption was refused.

Two prospective jurors asked how much they would be paid and whether it would jeopardize their relief and unemployment insurance benefits. One claimed exemption on the grounds that he would not make a suitable juror because he was a racist.

"Exemption refused. Don't worry, I shall find you an accused who is a racist."

At this point a very attractive, forthright, and confident woman, followed by a gowned, rather meek-looking attorney strode into the office, looked directly into my eyes, and asked, "What do you think about AIDS?"

"I am against all disease," I replied.

She continued, "I am the executive secretary of the vice-president of a large pharmaceutical company. If I am away from work, our entire AIDS research program will be stalled. Just last week the Minister of Health said how important it was to find a cure for AIDS."

She glanced at her attorney, who was trailing behind her.

Awed both by his client and by me, he coughed, looked sideways, returned to look at me imploringly and intoned, "It's true. It is very important that you exempt my client. Her employer is a large client of our offices and everything she says is correct."

She glared as I broke the bad news to her, "I cannot conceive of anyone more suitable to form part of a jury in a murder case than a person such as you who daily makes decisions affecting life and death. Exemption denied."

The woman left quickly. If looks could kill, she would have been charged with murder. Her attorney departed with less dispatch.

Juror 43 shook and trembled. He looked as if he was suffering from malaria. He sat down, tried to speak, but seemed unable to utter a syllable. I offered him a glass of water, which he sipped as he explained, "I am illiterate. I have been unable to sleep since I received the subpoena. I don't know if I can possibly be on a jury. I just got a job . . . " he babbled. "Do you know how hard it is to get a job when you cannot read? And I have a girlfriend. She said that if I can keep the job we might get married, and this is the first time that . . . "

"Exemption granted."

"I have not been able to find a job in two years, and . . . "

"Exemption granted, you can go. Good luck with your new job."

This time he understood. He rose and shook my hand, shook hands with the Crown attorney and the court clerk, shook hands with me a second time and left mumbling, "Thank you . . . thank you."

I granted an exemption to a mother with two children under three years of age at home and refused to exempt the candidate who was a volunteer fireman in the community where he owned a summer cottage.

Thirty-four people had requested exemptions. Eight were

granted, seventeen were refused, and nine members of the panel had their jury duty postponed to the subsequent term. The applications for exemption having been decided, I returned to the courtroom for jury selection.

It is a basic principle of criminal law that everything transpires in open court and in the presence of the accused. As a corollary of this principle, the judge is not allowed to have any private communication with members of the jury. At the beginning of the trial, the judge informs the jury that if they have a question or a problem, they should write it down and give it to one of their guards. The note is delivered to the judge, read aloud in open court, and then filed in the court record. The first messages from the jury usually request that the witness speak louder; others complain about the coffee machine, or request reserved parking spaces or the like.

In one of my first jury trials, I was startled when I received the following message fifteen minutes after the trial had begun:

URGENT! URGENT!
Juror Number 1 must wee wee!

I adjourned immediately to permit the juror to attend to his needs. The legal question was whether or not to read the message aloud and file it in the record. I decided to show it to the attorneys and the accused and file it without public reading.

The judge is responsible for the jury's welfare. All matters from the least significant to the most important are referred to him. He determines the hours of their sittings, their coffee breaks, where the jury will eat, whether they will be allowed to have a glass of wine with their meal, where they will sleep during their deliberations, and whether they should be denied access to newspapers and television. These are routine decisions that the judge makes easily.

At times, he becomes involved in their personal lives. Will he please provide the juror with a note for his professor at university to explain an absence from the exam-writing session. Should the juror be advised that a relative has died in a violent road accident? If the juror is to be advised, should this be done immediately or just before the funeral? Perhaps a verdict will be rendered before that time. Problems of illness arise. Police may be sent to a juror's home or a doctor's office to obtain certain medicines. A sick juror may be exempted.

Some problems begin as an individual concern and rapidly affect the entire jury. I recall one trial where by pure coincidence, a juror had parked her car in an outdoor lot next to the car of the son of the accused. When the court adjourned, they met and she became concerned that she was being followed. The following day, she expressed her fears to her fellow jurors and they all became skittish. Special measures were taken to provide reserved parking spaces for the jury and to arrange for uniformed guards to meet them each morning as they arrived at the courthouse parking lot and accompany them to the entrance. In spite of these precautions, I was concerned about my nervous jury. (Jurors are obliged to withstand substantial pressures and judge impartially; a nervous juror might not be able to take the pressure and might act in a way that would require him or her to be removed from the jury. If the number of jury members drops below ten, the judge must declare a mistrial.)

On Friday afternoon, as I left the courthouse, I observed the first nervous juror seated in an eight-year-old Chevrolet. Her fellow jurors and three uniformed guards were pushing the car, trying to get up enough speed for her to start the engine. As the car started with a cough and a spurt, she drove off into the distance. The jury had become a team working together. The crisis was over.

Few administrative matters receive as much attention during the trial as the jury's meals. Larger courthouses have restaurant facilities, but in smaller cities, the jury is led by their guards to a convenient restaurant in the vicinity of the courthouse for their lunchtime meal. After a few days, the jury will have eaten in all of the restaurants that are in any way suitable. They then begin to express a preference as to restaurants, which the judge tries to respect. As the trial continues, differences appear among the jurors, and arguments and votes are taken as to where they should all eat.

Some juries make outrageous demands. I have seen juries try to convert a murder trial into a gourmet experience at government expense. The judge begins to wonder how a jury that cannot agree whether to eat at "The Old Spaghetti House" or "St. Hubert BBQ" will ever decide unanimously on the guilt or innocence of the accused.

When the deliberations begin, judges, lawyers, and court officials try to divine the mood and inclinations of the jury from their appetites. Leftovers from meals eaten in the courthouse are studied like the entrails of a holy animal in the hope that they will yield a clue as to the progress being made in the deliberations. Various theories about this phenomenon have been expounded. Some are true, others are far-fetched, few are logical. I cannot give a scientific explanation, but must acknowledge the truth of the proposition that a jury that eats pizza in the courthouse is close to a verdict. Experienced observers know that when the pizza box appears, the verdict will soon follow.

It is not easy for a jury to agree on a verdict. As their deliberations progress, the judge and the attorneys watch the faces of the jurors as they enter the deliberation room in the morning, when they leave for a stroll or a meal, and at the end of the day. Their smiles disappear, their steps become heavy. As the discussions continue, they realize the magnitude of their task. Pressure mounts on those who do not share the view of the majority. Some give in, others resist. All become conscious that they are deciding the future of the accused.

When the jury has reached a unanimous decision, they send a note to the judge, saying, "We have a verdict."

Within minutes, he dons his gown and sends his usher to inform the waiting attorneys that court will reconvene shortly.

Most trials do not attract widespread attention and are sparsely attended. Yet when a jury is about to give a verdict, word spreads through the courthouse instantaneously. When the court reopens, about ten minutes after the note is received, it is filled with members of the public, the Press, lawyers who happen to be in the vicinity, and palace personnel.

Few experiences can rival the emotion and drama at this moment in the assizes. Television renditions of court decisions pale beside the real-life experience. Unparalleled tension prevails for the five or ten minutes between the moment a judge receives a note from the jury that they have agreed on a verdict and the time required to convene the court and complete the requisite formalities that precede the public declaration of guilt or innocence.

The judge enters the crowded, expectant, and hushed courtroom. The jury follows. Their faces are impassive. The accused is ordered to rise and the court clerk asks the prescribed questions.

"Have you chosen a forelady or foreman to speak on your behalf?"

"What is your verdict?"

The forelady or foreman announces the verdict.

At this point, in a television drama, attention focuses on the accused and the jury becomes irrelevant. The accused and his lawyer occupy centre stage. In the real world, the judge who receives a verdict of guilty from a jury in a murder trial worries about the jury. Others will attend to the accused.

The jury now appreciates the enormity of what they have done. They return to their deliberation room slowly, gather their belongings, and say farewell. Many are fearful, some are sick to their stomachs, a few are haunted by doubts that they may have done the wrong thing, and some are convinced that they decided correctly but nonetheless empathize with the accused. The judge enters the jury room for the first time. He shakes hands, reassures the jurors that their verdict is reasonable, and assuages their fears. The judge has descended from the Bench. He speaks to them directly, personally, and expresses the appreciation of a grateful society.

The remarks of the jurors are varied.

"You said this would be a unique experience. I didn't like it."

"Do you agree with our verdict?"

"Thank you for being there every time we looked up."

"I don't think I shall sleep well tonight."

"This is hard work."

"Can we go home now?"

"Did we make the decision you wanted?"

"What will happen to the accused now?"

A judge's first time presiding over a major criminal trial with a jury is a traumatic experience, a *rite de passage*. I admit to having had some doubts during my first jury trial. During the adjournments, I phoned more experienced colleagues frequently for advice and encouragement. When the trial was successfully completed, I was relieved. The following Wednesday, at the regular criminal law meeting of judges, I was queried about my experience.

"Well," I said, "I must have done something right. The accused is in jail and I am free."

What if the judge does not agree with the verdict of the jury? Well, the best rule is to keep quiet. If there is no evidence whatsoever implicating the accused, the judge can direct acquittal. If there is some evidence, the jury must decide. That is their role as judges of the facts. All a judge can do is remember the Magna Carta and allow the accused's fate to be determined by "the lawful judgment of his equals" — by the jurors who represent God and the country. Still, there are verdicts that are difficult to accept, and judges cannot always conceal their emotions.

When I first began sitting in the criminal division, my old friend Justice Mackay had elected to sit less often and would no longer preside in the criminal assizes. He presented me with his criminal law library as a gift. Among the volumes was a book containing standard jury charges. As I turned its pages, a note in his handwriting fell from between the pages. I lifted the paper from the floor and read, "Members of the jury, that is your verdict. I shall always be comforted by the knowledge that it is your verdict and not mine."

In criminal proceedings before a jury, the judge must determine what evidence is admissible. He cannot permit the jury to hear lengthy damaging testimony and then tell them to disregard what they heard. At times, the judge will hear part of the evidence outside the presence of the jury before deciding if the evidence may be presented. This mini-trial by the judge is called a *voir dire* and is often held to determine whether or not a statement made by the accused to a police officer is admissible. The judge who must determine the admissibility of a statement or confession is aware that the ultimate verdict may depend upon his decision. The *voir dire* of George Lawrence is a case in point.

The arrest of George Lawrence was most efficient. Lawrence was accused of having murdered his sweetheart's cocaine supplier. The girl's home was staked out and the police hoped that eventually Lawrence would make an appearance. When the team of officers conducting the surveillance tired, they phoned headquarters for a replacement team. Two other agents were dispatched.

While driving to the location for their assignment, the officers proceeded along Viau Street, where they found Lawrence standing on the side of the road, trying to hitch a ride. He was arrested and brought to police headquarters, where he was questioned at length and eventually signed a confession.

At trial, Lawrence sought to repudiate the confession and claimed to have been mistreated, but his denial rang hollow after the police testified. The arresting officer said, "After he signed the confession, he stood up, shook our hands, and said, 'This was a damn good investigation. Good work, you guys are real pros.'"

Lawrence admitted making the comments. When asked to explain his conduct and remarks, he responded, "I said it because they were gentlemen."

Needless to say, I admitted the confession, despite the vigorous arguments of his attorney that it was not free and voluntary.

Justice André Gervais once conducted a *voir dire* to determine if a confession by the accused had been freely made without promises or threats by the police officers. The accused had refused counsel and insisted on defending himself. "I signed the confession," he explained, "because the police beat me. I was so badly injured that I had to go to the hospital for an autopsy."

The judge couldn't resist. "Your testimony would be more credible," he said, "if you would file your death certificate as an exhibit."

Once I presided over a *voir dire* involving two drug dealers who were viciously murdered. When their bodies were found in an abandoned Jeep in the woods north of Laval near Montreal, the police launched an intensive search for the killers. The evidence pointed to "Joker" Boyer, a small-time hash dealer who was well known to the police. The initial efforts to locate Joker were fruitless, but he was finally located, placed under continuing surveillance, and followed to a motel in the Laurentian Mountains northwest of the city.

After three days of observation, the police prepared to make their move. To ensure maximum surprise, the arrest was scheduled for six o'clock in the morning. At five o'clock, nine members of the SWAT team and the investigators met for a briefing. They then drove to the motel and met the surveillance team. Proceeding with clockwork precision, three members of the SWAT team, with machine guns drawn, burst into Room 17. To their surprise it was empty.

The police were undaunted. A rapid verification established that there had been an innocent error. The fugitive was really in Unit 21 and the assault was re-launched. This time several members of the SWAT team removed the outside door from its hinges while other armed members of the raiding party stormed the room. It was occupied, but not by Joker Boyer. When police questioned the occupant, he told them that Joker was lodged in Room 26.

Once again the SWAT team and investigators set off in search of their man. This time the police were more circumspect. The investigators stayed behind at a safe distance. The captain of the SWAT team knocked on the door and shouted, "Joker, you're under arrest. Come out with your arms raised!"

Inside the motel room Joker had been sleeping soundly, naked as a jaybird. Awakened by the shouts and fearing for his life, he got out of bed and without pausing to dress, opened the door. His nude figure faced two machine guns. Within seconds he was forced to lie down on the gravel passage, and his arms were cuffed behind his back. The investigators then came forward, pulled him to his feet, and read him his rights.

At trial, the principal investigator was asked to describe the arrest. When he completed the description of the events, the Crown attorney inquired, "When you approached the accused, what did you observe?"

The reply was as simple as it was true.

"Joker was not armed."

Michael Donovan Cushing had never heard of the Magna Carta, Runnymede, or King John. His knowledge of English history was nonexistent and he could barely name the last five presidents of the United States. But he knew that if you rolled dice and the number five appeared, the concealed number was a two. Although he lived in Harlem with his divorced wife Sally and their child, he knew every stop on the train from New York to Trenton, New Jersey. He knew how to buy and sell coke on the streets of Harlem and he knew that Canada was a country to the north that he would like to visit. When the opportunity presented itself, he happily joined a friend for a short trip in a borrowed car.

The excursion did not turn out as planned. A few miles after they crossed the Canadian border into Quebec, the car was stopped and searched. The police found 27 grams of cocaine, and both were arrested and charged with possession of cocaine for the purpose of trafficking. Their protestations of innocence were ignored, and after a brief trial, each was sentenced to eighteen months in jail.

Jail would not have been so bad if Cushing had been sent to an institution in Montreal or Ontario, but he ended up in Chicoutimi, where the only English-speaking person he knew was his travelling companion, accomplice, and fellow prisoner.

Police officers and representatives of the Canadian immigration service paid him periodic visits to ask a few questions about his parents and place of birth, but Cushing didn't know the answers to their questions. As far as he knew, he had been born in New York. He had no recollection of his parents. The first person he could remember was the white storekeeper with whom he had lived. They didn't believe him. Over and over again, they asked:

"Who was your mother?"

"Where was you birth registered?"

"Who was your father?"

"Where did you live after you were born?"

"Don't you have any family? Brothers? Sisters? Aunts, uncles? Anyone to whom you are related? Why not?"

The answer was always "no." After each ten-minute interview, the police or immigration officer would leave without further explanation. Life in prison was dull, but at least the visits interrupted the monotony.

He had little to do with the other prisoners. They spoke no English and made little effort to communicate with him in sign language. He was big, and strong enough to discourage unwanted attention. Occasionally he would be permitted to use the public pay phone — an opportunity that he welcomed, even though he knew his conversations would be overheard by the guards. To phone his old friends in New York, all he had to do was dial the number of the public phone on the street in front of Sally's flat. Anyone who happened to walk by would answer, accept the charges, and try to find Sally. If they failed to locate her on the first shout, there was always someone else who would speak to him. Nothing was said that would get him into trouble, but it was nice to hear some real New York English.

Cushing expected to be released after he'd served a third of his sentence. He counted the days and said all the right things when he was interviewed.

"Yes, I want to return to New York."

"No, I would never return to Canada."

"I'm sorry. I didn't know there was coke in the car."

"I know that coke is illegal and won't touch the stuff."

"I still love Sally, even though we're divorced. Besides, we had a kid together and I want to see my little girl."

"No, I never raped anyone. Why the hell should I, when there are so many women available?"

"No, I've never been to Jamaica. Why would I want to go there anyway? It's hot enough in New York."

The days dragged on. Six months passed and he wasn't paroled. His friend was released, but he remained in jail, unable to understand a system of justice that sentenced two men to jail for eighteen months for the same offence, released one after six months, and kept the other one in jail without explanation. But then, government and cops usually foul these things up. It wasn't the first time in his life that he'd got the short end of the stick — or was this the long end?

Ten months passed. The immigration officers kept visiting and asking the same questions, but he could not give them any more information. He could never understand why they kept hounding him for a birth certificate and repeated those questions. Finally, he asked and was told that the American authorities would not let him go back home until the Canadian police proved that he was a United States citizen and they needed his birth certificate to prove that he'd been born in New York.

He told them of his few years at school, but they weren't able to find a record of his attendance. He described his teachers and even mentioned a few classmates. It didn't help. All they had to do was look at him, speak to him about the streets of New York, the bars, clubs, the Yankees, Central Park, Harlem, the train to Jersey and they would know he was American. The law works in strange ways. It ignores a man without a passport.

A year passed. Still, he was not paroled, and he began to lose patience. He said as much to his friends who answered the sidewalk pay phone. Two weeks later the prison authorities intercepted a package containing a pair of running shoes sent to him by a friend. They X-rayed the shoes and found a file concealed in the soles. Further inquiry established that a small light aircraft had been chartered to transport him back to the United States after he completed his escape from prison. The authorities briefly considered letting Cushing escape, but the prospect was too dangerous. A guard or other inmate might be injured during the break-out, they thought. It never occurred to them that the easiest way to get rid of their guest who had overstayed his welcome would be to set him free and leave him to his own devices to gain entry to the U.S.

The American authorities denied that Cushing was a U.S. citizen and suggested that he was a Jamaican native. They claimed he was wanted in the United States on a rape charge but did not request that he be extradited. Frequent phone calls were exchanged between the police and immigration officials in both Canada and the United States, but nothing materialized, and Cushing remained in jail. He served his entire sentence.

On the day that he was to be released, the federal immigration officers were waiting for him at the prison gates. They placed him in the back of their car and informed him that though he had served his full term, they were afraid he would run away and hide before he could be deported and that he would be held in another prison in Montreal until he cooperated and provided them with the information required so he could obtain a passport and be deported. He was taken to Parthenais Jail in Montreal. The routine weekly interviews with the immigration officials resumed. Two months later a legal aid lawyer met Cushing and prepared the application for a writ of Habeas Corpus.

On the first day in court, Cushing was scared. He had been in prison for twenty-one months and knew that he would never be able to obtain a passport, at least not as long as he was stuck in a Canadian jail. He entered the courtroom wearing jeans and a green undershirt. His eyes were sullen, his wrists handcuffed, and his legs in irons. Hell, he had served his time, and they were still treating him like a criminal.

175

The Crown, who were obliged to justify Cushing's detention, coolly presented the testimony of the police and immigration officers. They had complied with all the technical legal requirements, conducted weekly interrogations, and blamed this state of affairs on Cushing's failure to satisfactorily explain his birth. But when Cushing testified, a torrent of information poured forth.

For a day and a half he told and retold his life story, answering all questions at great length. I listened impassively and realized that the entire machinery of government was keeping Cushing in jail because they wanted to deport him to the United States. Cushing's sole desire was to return to his native New York. The solution was simple. Free this man and the problem would be solved.

This was a violation of Article 29 of Magna Carta and virtually every subsequent constitution, code of criminal law, and charter of rights. This was the very essence of Habeas Corpus. Produce the prisoner and justify his detention. The detention was unjustified. I ordered his immediate release.

The government appealed my order. The Court of Appeal shared my outrage at the continued imprisonment of Cushing and confirmed my order. He was finally released.

Two days later, the police and immigration officers lost contact with him, and later that month his attorney called to tell me privately that Michael Donovan Cushing was back on the streets of New York. When I met the attorney in the entrance to the courthouse some time afterwards, he told me his client had such great respect for the court that had ordered his release that he was seriously considering applying to the immigration authorities for permission to enter Canada as a landed immigrant.

And all of this thanks to King John.

IV

Plays, Pleasant and Unpleasant

11

Euclid

Euclid Brodeur stared at the traffic light as it turned green, orange, red, and then green again. He was sitting in his car on the highway south of Montreal, but could not remember why he was there or what he had done. He glanced at the pistol on the seat beside him and slowly picked it up. The barrel smelled of gunpowder and had obviously been fired recently. He thought hard but could not remember what had happened. He had left the house to visit his daughter. She lived with her mother in the adjacent town. He could remember leaving his house, and after that everything was blank. Could he have harmed his young daughter, Natalie? No, that was impossible. He must have killed his wife. He must tell the police and they would investigate. Slowly, he turned left and headed off in the direction of the police station. They would understand and they would investigate. They would find his daughter and make sure she had not been harmed.

The sun shone in his eyes as he drove up to the station and parked his car. He stepped out, walked to the door, and knocked. No one answered. It was only four-thirty in the afternoon; surely the officer on duty hadn't left for the day already. There must have been an emergency. Who ever heard of the police station being closed in the middle of the day? Well, it was no stranger than his being unable to recall where he had been and what he had done. He went back to his car and drove home.

From his apartment he phoned the police. Someone picked up at the other end, "Sûreté du Québec, can I help you?"

"Yes, I think I killed someone . . . my wife. Please send a policeman."

"Who is speaking? Please reply slowly with your name and address."

"My name is Euclid Brodeur. I live at 37 Montée Drummondville."

"We will send a car to your home immediately. We will also call an ambulance," said the voice.

"No, you do not understand. My wife does not live with me. She lives at 149 Chemin Chambly. Please send a car to her house. Please find my daughter. I'm worried."

"Stay where you are. Our men will be there shortly. I shall radio a car in the vicinity of your wife's home. Do not go anywhere. It is important that you stay where you are and do not touch anything. Do you understand me?"

"Yes, I do. I will not go out. But please find my daughter. I don't know what I did."

"Don't worry. We will investigate and we will find your daughter."

"Thank you," replied Euclid. As he was putting the receiver down, there was a knock and a voice called, "Euclid Brodeur. This is the Sûreté du Québec. Open the door."

He got up and unlatched the front door of his apartment. Two uniformed policemen came in. The first officer told him to raise his hands and face the wall, and searched him. His partner made a rapid tour of the apartment. He could not help but notice the gun on the bedroom dresser.

"Is that your gun?"

"Yes," he replied.

"Mr. Brodeur. We are not sure what happened. We were instructed to come here and stay with you while other officers checked your wife's home. In the meantime, we must warn you that we are investigating a possible murder. You are entitled to consult a lawyer immediately. You have the right to remain silent. Anything you say may be used in court against you."

At that moment the phone rang. As Euclid rose to answer, one police officer put a hand on his shoulder to stop him. The other officer answered, listened for a moment, then said to Euclid, "Monsieur Brodeur, you are under arrest for the murder of your wife, Christine Brodeur. I must now repeat the warning I gave you previously . . . "

Euclid's mind wandered off, then he looked up and asked, "My daughter. What about Natalie?"

"We have not found her. Have you any idea where she may be?"

"Yes. She has a friend, Emilie Blais, who lives nearby. They often visit. They are friends."

"We will look for her. But now you must come with us to the station. Take your belongings and let's go. You may have to stay a while."

The three men rose. One of the officers picked up the pistol and placed it in a plastic bag. When they got into the police car, he asked, "Mr. Brodeur, would you like to stop for a cup of coffee?"

"I am not hungry," Euclid replied. "Whatever you want. I am not in a hurry. But will they be able to call you when they find my daughter?"

"Yes, the cellular phone between the car seats works well and we have our radio."

"Perhaps a cup of coffee would be good."

They drove silently to the McDonald's restaurant on the side of the highway, parked the police car, and got out. One of the officers stayed with Euclid at an outside table, while the other walked to the counter and ordered three hamburgers, french fries, and coffee. He returned, and the police officers started eating their food. Euclid looked on absent-mindedly and sipped his coffee two or three times.

At the station Euclid was fingerprinted, photographed, and searched again. This time they took his tie, his belt, and the contents of his pockets and put them in a bag. They offered him another cup of coffee and asked him if he wanted to say anything. He shook his head from side to side.

"Please find Natalie, and I shall tell you anything you want to know."

The officer left the room. When he returned, he smiled at Euclid and said, "Your daughter is safe. She was with her friend, Emilie. She said that she was waiting for you to pick her up but you did not appear."

"That must be true," said Euclid. "I shall tell you what happened, but I do not remember much after I left my house. But what of my wife? Is she dead? Oh yes, she must be. I am under arrest for her murder."

A second officer entered the room before Euclid had a chance to say more, "Wait a moment. If Euclid wants to make a statement, get him a legal aid lawyer. I'm tired of having statements thrown out at trial. Mr. Brodeur, do you have a lawyer?"

"No."

"Well, you're lucky. André Lesage is the legal aid lawyer on duty tonight. Shall I call so you can speak to him before you make a statement?"

"Okay, I think I've heard his name. I'll speak to him."

The officer placed the call. When Lesage answered, he gave the phone to Euclid, and both officers withdrew from the office. They continued to watch Euclid through a large glass window but could not hear his words. After four or five minutes, Euclid replaced the receiver and the officers re-entered the room.

"Do you still want to make a statement?"

"Yes, I'll tell you everything. Then I want to speak to my daughter."

"Fine. Please speak slowly so we can write it all down; we're not secretaries."

Euclid spoke for an hour. After leaving school at the age of fourteen he had worked as a plumber's helper. Life had not been easy. He gave all the money he earned to his father as payment for room and board. At the age of nineteen, he became a licensed plumber and got a job at the food processing plant near his home maintaining their equipment and building. Euclid was proud of the fact that he had worked for the same company for twenty-seven years. They have given him special mention at the Christmas party two years ago.

He had married Christine at the age of twenty and they had five children, the oldest of whom was twenty-six. His wife had been pregnant when they were wed, and the other children had arrived at two-year intervals. That is, all except their youngest daughter, who now lived with her mother. Life had not been easy. Christine became depressed after the birth of their third child and from that time until their divorce four years ago, she had spent frequent periods in the hospital.

The divorce had been bad. He loved Christine and could not imagine why she wanted a divorce, but Marc, his oldest son, had encouraged her to leave him. It was so lonely after Christine left and took Marc and Natalie with her. From time to time, he still saw Robert and Suzanne, but Marc had turned against him and did not even talk to him.

It was no doubt Marc who had suggested that his mother see that lawyer. When Christine had sued for divorce he had been obliged to go to Court for the first time in his life. It was not pleasant: the crowds, the waiting, the day lost from work, and then the judgment that ordered him to pay alimony. He had to pay $125 a week for Christine and Natalie. The others didn't need support.

Of course there was Pauline, his oldest daughter. Poor Pauline had been sick like her mother. As a teenager she had taken drugs and become so sick that she was hospitalized for a long time, then went to live in an institution. He visited her as often as possible, but last summer, Pauline had died. She took her own life in the special school where she lived. It had been terrible. Pauline had never told him to go away or that she loved her mother more. If only Pauline had been well, he would have gotten along with her. Well, now it was too late. Pauline was dead.

Shortly before Pauline's death, his wife's lawyer had sent him more of those papers about the divorce. This time the lawyer wanted the alimony increased to $200 a week, which was more than Euclid could afford. He did not earn enough money and would be forced into debt. He had been working since the age of fourteen and had never owed anyone a penny. The thought was unbearable.

At Pauline's funeral, Euclid decided to resolve the problem with his wife. He walked over to her at the cemetery. She was standing beside Marc, who refused even to acknowledge his presence. But Euclid spoke to Christine anyway and invited her to come with him for a coffee after the burial. She did not resist when he put his arms around her. Later that afternoon, they sat in Dunkin' Donuts discussing their lost daughter. Euclid broached the subject of the alimony and explained how he could not pay her $200 a week. If she would agree to continue to receive $125, he would give her an additional $25 a week in cash, tax free. Christine agreed. Later in the afternoon, he drove her back to her home.

Well, he had settled his financial problems, but the case

was not over. He didn't tell his lawyer of the settlement with Christine because he thought he would be angry. The lawyer had said to leave everything in his hands. Perhaps Christine had failed to tell her lawyer for the same reason. In any event, when he went to Court the judge ordered him to pay alimony of $200 a week.

Euclid did not go to work the next day. He just wandered around thinking about his financial problems. Twice he went to the Caisse Populaire and withdrew $25 from his account, asking the teller each time to check his balance. He joked with her and said he hoped there was enough money in his account. Once, while waiting in line, he met an old friend and told him about the Court and the judge.

"The judge has given his sentence," Euclid said, "but I have not given mine."

At four that afternoon, he went to work and explained to the foreman that he had been sick earlier. He asked about the possibility of a raise, but times were tough, and the foreman said that though a raise could perhaps be given at the end of the year, it would not be feasible before then. Besides, there was the union contract.

Euclid went back home and fell asleep while sitting in his favourite chair watching TV. When he awoke at three in the morning the TV set was still on, but all he saw was the blank, speckled screen. He shut off the TV and went to bed. The next morning his mind was made up. He would have to kill his wife. There was no other solution.

He remembered going to work that morning and returning home early. This was the day he would drive to his wife's home and take Natalie to McDonald's for dinner. He took the pistol that he kept near his bed, went down to his car, and . . . the next thing he knew, he was stopped at that traffic light. His mind was a blank.

Several hours later, when the police officer asked him to read the typed statement, he signed without reading a word.

It didn't matter. He would spend the rest of his life in jail and would not be able to return to work.

In the morning, he met his lawyer, André Lesage. The police had wanted him to speak with their doctor and Lesage had another doctor who would see him. Well, if that was what they wanted, he would cooperate. He had always been a law-abiding citizen and did not owe any money. He met both the police psychiatrist and the woman psychiatrist sent by his lawyer. Both asked the same questions over and over. They wanted to know every detail about his wife's illness, his daughter's death, his fight with his son Marc. It was not a fight. He and Marc just did not speak to each other.

The trial began two months later, with Lesage entering a plea of not guilty on behalf of his client. The defence would be insanity. The early part of the trial was uneventful and drew little attention. The statement signed by Euclid was presented as evidence. According to the police witnesses, there were tracks from the tires of Euclid's car in front of his wife's home and the bullet removed from the dead body had been fired from Euclid's pistol.

The officers traced Euclid's movements throughout the forty-eight-hour period preceding the killing. The waitress in the restaurant where he ate, the teller in the Caisse Populaire, the friend he had met in line, his foreman at work, all testified.

Euclid sat on the hard bench in the prisoner's dock, flanked by two police officers. He watched silently, un-comprehending. Why were they conducting this elaborate trial? It was obvious — at least to him — that he had killed his wife. He had not received this much attention in his entire life. Why now? The trial went on and on and on, and Euclid just sat and watched. When the Court adjourned for a brief period, he would be taken to the small cell in the rear of the dock. The food was better than in the prison, and the guards were nice. One played cards with him during the lunch break.

The most difficult part was when his children testified. He heard Marc tell how his father had hit him with a ruler when he was young. Marc had told his mother to move out with Natalie because his father was a violent man. That was not true. The other children were less critical when they testified. One said that he had never harmed his wife, at least not until the day of her death. Euclid loved his wife. He must have killed her but could not remember.

The doctors testified for a long time, using many words that Euclid could not understand. Both agreed that his amnesia was genuine. The mind wipes out events it cannot tolerate. The police doctor said that Euclid knew what he intended to do, had knowingly driven his car to his wife's home, and after the shooting his mind erased his memory from the time he left his apartment until the time he arrived at the traffic light.

The defence psychiatrist said almost the same thing, with only one difference. She thought that the accumulation of shocks — the death of his daughter, the rejection by Marc, the departure of his wife and Natalie, the repudiation of the settlement of the alimony claim, and the judgment increasing the alimony from $125 to $200 created a pressure Euclid could not resist. When the dam broke, he lost control and drifted into a disassociative state. For a brief period, his mind no longer directed his body. He suffered a form of temporary alienation.

The more the doctors spoke, the less Euclid understood. He began to hope that the trial would just end. He knew that he would never be able to return to work and the proof had convinced him that he had murdered his wife.

A casual observer, newspaper reader, or television viewer who was given a brief summary of the trial would readily conclude that Euclid was guilty of murder and might wonder why the deliberations were so long. But the jury and I knew differently. Euclid was not a name in a headline, he was a man trapped by circumstances he could not control or understand. He had killed his wife and yet appeared as a victim. The jury was asked to minutely examine and weigh two days and one fatal event. They knew the story of Euclid's past and would determine his future.

This was the tragedy of a frail, simple man who had caused the death of the wife he loved while still mourning the loss of his favourite child. If Euclid were found guilty, it would be a further plague on this unfortunate family. Yet he had killed his wife.

The jury deliberations continued. They sent notes to me and requested additional instructions on the meaning of intention. They requested and listened to the tapes of the waitress in the restaurant and the friend in the Caisse Populaire who had heard Euclid mention that he had not yet rendered his sentence. They asked a further question on the difference between murder and manslaughter. Again, I explained the concepts of intentional homicide or murder and unintentional homicide by unlawful acts, which we call manslaughter.

Throughout the proceedings, both the attorney for the Crown and André Lesage waited for the verdict in the courtroom and the adjacent corridor. I wandered back and forth between my office and the public corridor. It was hard to concentrate on the case reports that I had brought along to read. The theory that Euclid was temporarily insane had not convinced me. After all, he had known that he intended to eliminate his problem and had said as much to a few people. The jury would have trouble finding him guilty of second-degree murder because they would feel sorry and seek a compromise verdict. His stress would be a factor. They might consider that despite the gun, the killing was unintended and find him guilty of manslaughter. Acquittal, however, seemed out of the question.

If Euclid were found guilty of second-degree murder, the sentence would be imprisonment for life with no possibility of parole before he had served ten years of his jail term. But should the jury find him guilty of manslaughter, I, alone, would have to determine the sentence. For this crime, the law establishes a range of punishment from immediate release to life in prison. Release was inconceivable; he had killed his wife. A judge may enjoy great discretion, even latitude, but the exercise of discretion must not yield an arbitrary result. The sentence must be consistent with other decisions. Public perception and reaction have to be considered. The sentence should dissuade the accused and others from further crime. Homicide cannot be condoned.

But in every sentence there is a subjective element. Euclid had already sentenced himself to a life without the woman he loved, remote and isolated from his children. He would not survive a long prison term. Nevertheless, my respect for precedent and consideration for public perception would not permit me to impose a sentence of less than five years.

A number of senior citizens waited in the hallway. This was the regular audience that attended all trials in the area. They know the lawyers and the court officials. Occasionally they place small bets on the outcome of the proceedings, and the date and time of the verdict.

After three days of deliberation by the jury, the guard delivered a note to me: "We have a verdict." Within minutes the lawyers, police officers, spectators, and court officials had reassembled in the courtroom.

"Ladies and gentlemen of the jury, have you selected a forelady or foreman who will speak for you?"

"We have."

"How do you find the accused?"

"We find the accused not guilty by reason of insanity."

Without pausing, I said, "The Court accepts your verdict and orders that it be recorded." Turning to the prisoner, I continued, "Euclid Brodeur, you have been found 'not guilty by reason of insanity' by a jury of your peers. I order that you be detained at the pleasure of the government. You will be kept in an institution for the mentally ill, until the government is satisfied that you are cured and can resume your place in society safely. This Court is adjourned."

Two weeks later, while walking downtown, I encountered my old friend, Arnold. He smiled and told me he had heard of Euclid's trial.

"How did you hear about it?" I asked. "It wasn't especially newsworthy and wasn't written up in the papers."

"My French teacher. His wife was the psychiatrist for the defence. She never thought the jury would acquit."

I hadn't either.

I never considered how Euclid would react to life in a mental institution after having seen his wife and daughter suffer the agonies of depression and mental illness. Now, he who had cared for and visited them would be surrounded by constant reminders of their experience. He would have been better off in the local prison, but that was beyond my power.

A year later I returned to the palace where Euclid had been tried. André Lesage must have had a trial that day. He greeted me in the corridor.

"How is Euclid?" I asked. "Have the doctors made a report about his possible release?"

"No, *Monsieur le juge*," he responded, "Euclid never made it to the mental institution. These facilities are overcrowded and he could not be admitted. He is still in our local jail waiting for a transfer. I hope he'll be released in a year or so."

Circumstances rendered the judgment that reason would have denied my heart.

12

The Charge

For the trial of this charge of murder, Joey Gordon has placed himself upon God and his Country, whom you represent. For almost eight hundred years, an accused has enjoyed the right to be tried by a jury of his peers, a jury of his equals. You are the equals of the accused, chosen to decide this case . . . "

The seven men and five women on the jury had been pulled from their routine to try the case. Most of them had heard of the murder on the radio or seen the accused on TV. In a small town people talk about these things, especially when they happen on the reserve only a few miles away, and stories of native claims, blocked roads, and violence are hot in the media these days. So when a native Canadian comes before the court, it is a public affair.

The jury on this case looked particularly young; only one member was more than forty. Juror number five was to be married the next month, but I had assured him the trial would be brief and his wedding plans would not be disrupted. The attorneys completed their arguments and I was now delivering my charge. Juror number five would be released several weeks before his wedding date. The question was whether Joey Gordon would be released, ever. He was charged with the murder of his neighbour, Charlie "Scattered Dust" Morris.

I had expected the choice of a jury to be difficult. How can twelve white men and women living in small towns and villages on the outskirts of Montreal be the equals of Joey? Could they appreciate living conditions on the reserve? Is it possible to imagine life in an unheated home on a windswept, deserted island? Scattered Dust and Joey were the only residents of Two Mile Island. They lived in the only two homes on the island. Joey rented his brother's house for $75 a month. It was equipped with electricity, some indoor plumbing, and an oil heater. The oil heater helped during the long winter, but there were plenty of drafts. Although there was a sink in the kitchen and an old tub in the bathroom, neither Joey nor his brother had ever bothered to install a toilet. It is not a simple matter to install plumbing on a barren island. You have to dig a cesspool, spread perforated pipes under the ground, and cover them with sand and gravel. It wasn't easy, so it wasn't done. But even though the house didn't have a toilet, it was still better than the other home on the island.

Scattered Dust didn't have electricity. He couldn't raise the thousand dollars the electric company required before they would connect his house to the transformer. Last summer, Joey helped him string a wire between the two homes, and he enjoyed the benefits of electricity for the first time, but when winter came, Joey disconnected the wire. He was afraid Scattered Dust would hook up the small portable heater he had purchased, and heaters consume a lot of power. The situation might have been different if Scattered Dust had offered to share the cost, but if he had had money, he could have arranged for his own electrical entry — or more likely, he would not even be living on this forsaken island with Joey as his only neighbour. Joey and Scattered Dust talked about electricity frequently. There wasn't much else to talk about.

In the summer, people from the mainland would visit — especially kids who liked to go out to the island to play baseball. They left their mitts and bats in Joey's shed. There were always boats around, and it wasn't difficult to row the three hundred yards from the mainland to the island. Winter wasn't too bad either. After the river froze, people walked to the island in their big boots and snowshoes. The kids skied over. In the spring and fall, there were fewer visitors because people were afraid of falling into the freezing water or getting their boats stuck in the ice.

It was early January. The fall weather had been mild and the ice had arrived late. Joey needed a few days off the island, so on Friday afternoon he crossed to the mainland in his motorboat to meet Dave Roundpoint, who had invited him to spend the night. Dave had a job as night watchman at a construction site where a house had been vandalized a few times. The house was equipped with a radio, two cots, and an old bridge table, several chairs, and a bottle of vodka. They camped out in the living room of the new home and talked and drank and drank through the long night. January is the worst time of year. It's dark, cold, and depressing, but Dave was a good guy, always prepared to share with his friends. They talked and drank the night away.

Joey had intended to buy supplies the next morning and return to the island, but that proved impossible. During the night, ice had formed in the river, and he spent the morning hacking at the ice to free his boat. The motor wouldn't start, so he towed it to his brother's garage with a borrowed pickup truck and trailer, planning to come back and fix the motor some other time. The next day he would return to the island in his brother's small rowboat. It would not be an easy crossing, but he had done it a thousand times before.

"You have taken an oath to carefully consider all the evidence and to render a verdict based on all the facts. You should study all the exhibits, read all the documents and reports, examine all the testimony of the witnesses, including the accused, who chose to testify. Decide what you will believe and what you will reject. You are free to believe all or part or none of the testimony of a witness. Use your common sense. The part of the evidence that you choose to believe is fact . . . "

Joey spent Saturday night at his brother's house. It was a cold night, and the wind howled and blew the snow about. Robert was a rich man who owned a centrally heated house, a pickup truck, and the small garage. He sold gas to the occasional passerby and in his spare time did miscellaneous repairs to car and boat engines. His wife and children had left the reserve years earlier with another man and he had grown accustomed to his solitary life. When his family had lived with him, they had used the home on the island in the summertime. Now that they were gone, he rented it to Joey. The rent wasn't much, but he wanted to keep the house on the island and there was no way that one man could afford to keep two homes.

Robert's house and garage backed onto the river. On a dark, clear night, he could look from his bedroom window and see lights on the island, though he couldn't quite distinguish the house. Joey paid him $75 a month for the house plus taxes and electricity. Nine hundred a year wasn't much, but the house was small and needed repairs, and Joey didn't bother him. The money was tax free. Joey received a government pension and paid him in cash when the monthly pension cheque arrived.

The morning after Joey's visit, he lent his brother his rowboat, along with some ropes with heavy steel hooks, a pick, and a long-handled spade. If Joey had a problem, he could throw the hooks ahead and pull on the ropes so the boat would slide through the channel or over the ice. The pick and spade could be used to break the ice and release the boat.

Joey took the bag with his belongings, a half-gallon of vodka that he had bought the previous day, and a few supplies, and set out for the island. The crossing was slow but he had no unexpected problems, even though it was a lot of hard work to break the ice, throw the hooks ahead, and pull the boat forward an inch at a time. It didn't help that Joey was not particularly strong. He was short, stocky, and though he was only forty-eight, had lost much of the strength of his youth. He probably drank too much, but what else could he do on those long winter nights?

It was four o'clock when he arrived back on the island. The sun was setting behind thick clouds and night had started to creep in. Joey dragged the boat onto the shore, turned it over, and placed the oars, spade, pick, and ropes under the boat to protect them from the snow. He trekked up to the house and entered. The oil heater was still working and the house was warm enough. This surprised him because the carburetor on the oil heater needed cleaning and adjustment. He lay down on the bed and fell asleep with his clothes on.

"You have sworn to decide this case solely on the evidence. You must set aside anything you may have read or heard outside this courtroom. Forget all preconceived notions, all prejudices, all impressions gathered from friends and relatives. Concentrate on the evidence and only on the evidence, so you may establish the facts, and reach a verdict based solely on these facts . . . ."

After sleeping for several hours, Joey rose from his bed and groped for the switch to turn on the sixty-watt lightbulb that hung from the ceiling. He wanted something to eat and thought he might grab a bite with Scattered Dust, whom he had not seen for several days. Joey dressed and walked the several hundred feet towards the white smoke that drifted from Scattered Dust's chimney.

Scattered Dust sat alone at his table, facing a glass and a

half-filled bottle containing an orange liquid. Premixed screwdriver was Scattered Dust's favourite drink. He gestured to Joey, who took a glass from the counter and joined him at the table. The men drank quietly, oblivious to each other's presence. After a while they began to speak, and Joey described his night on the mainland with Roundpoint guarding the construction site. The mention of construction caught the attention of Scattered Dust. He asked Joey if he could connect the electric wire to his house for the winter, and promised to make arrangements with the electric company for his own entry in the spring. In the meantime, however, he needed to hook up to Joey's home, or it would be a long, cold winter.

Joey stalled, nattered, and tried unsuccessfully to distract him. Finally, he told Scattered Dust that his brother Robert objected to any electrical connection, and since Robert owned the house he could not antagonize him. At that moment, the bottle of screwdriver gave out. Joey grunted and offered to go home and get the bottle of vodka he had purchased on the mainland. He hoped Scattered Dust would forget about the electric connection, have a few more drinks, and fall asleep. That was the way most of their arguments ended. A few more drinks and a long sleep would solve the problem for a while.

"You have taken an oath to keep your deliberations secret, both during and after the trial. This is to protect you from inquiring strangers and to encourage free and open discussions between the members of the jury. Remember, you need not account to any one but your own conscience, you need not be concerned with the consequences of your decision. Just examine the evidence and decide the innocence or guilt of the accused . . . "

Joey returned fifteen minutes later clutching his half-gallon of vodka. Scattered Dust produced a bottle of orange juice and they started drinking again in silence. Suddenly Scattered Dusk sat up straight, pointed to a rifle leaning against the corner of the room, and warned Joey that if he didn't agree to the electrical hook-up, he would shoot his head off and teach him why and how he had earned the name Scattered Dust.

Alarmed, Joey stood up, put on his toque, grabbed his vodka bottle from the table, and began to leave. Scattered Dust thrust out his arm with glass in hand and blocked the passage to the door. Without a word, Joey filled the glass with vodka, walked around him, and went back home. He decided he'd fix the carburetor on the oil stove, and then have a long, warm sleep. He walked into the house through the shed, placed the bottle of vodka on the table, removed his jacket, and began working on the oil heater.

The house was more comfortable this year. The new oil heater actually heated the entire house. The old one had been much smaller and inefficient, and only heated the living room. It also helped that Joey had filled the holes around the cement-block foundation where the cold air entered. For years, he had been collecting a pile of manure across from his home to use as fertilizer for a small garden, but he'd never got around to doing anything about it. In November, he decided it was more important to be warm in winter than to have vegetables in summer, so using his old wheelbarrow, he had spread the manure around the foundation.

Joey kept working on the carburetor. It was clogged with dirt but could be fixed in a few minutes. He removed it and put it on the table in the living room. Slowly and deliberately, he cleaned each part with a vodka-soaked cloth, reassembled the carburetor, and returned to the heater to put it back in place. When the job was complete, he pushed the restart button, and the heater began working again. It sounded much better.

"The first principle of law which you must apply throughout this trial and your deliberations is that the accused is presumed innocent until the evidence adduced has convinced you of his guilt beyond a

197

reasonable doubt. The accused need not prove anything; he need not tender any evidence. The prosecution must bear the burden of proof and prove beyond a reasonable doubt that the crime was committed, the accused was the perpetrator of the criminal act, and that the defence offered does not lie . . . ."

Joey heard the shed door open. It was Scattered Dust, clutching a bottle of orange juice. He must have gotten over his anger, or at least his thirst must have been greater than his rage. Joey rose from behind the heater, the two men sat down at the table, and they started drinking vodka and orange juice again. Before long the subject of the electrical connection arose once more. Joey explained again that it was not his decision but his brother's. To convince Scattered Dust, he picked up the phone and called Robert, but Robert was in no mood to be disturbed and refused to speak to either of them. He told Joey to send Scattered Dust home and to stop bothering him in the middle of the night. Joey passed along the message, got up, and went outside to relieve himself. In a few minutes, he returned . . .

"Joey Gordon is charged with the second-degree murder of Charlie "Scattered Dust" Morris. You and only you can decide if the death was caused by a criminal act, if Joey Gordon committed the criminal act, and whether the defence is unfounded. Remember, it is the burden of the prosecution to convince you beyond a reasonable doubt . . . "

The Mohawk police had not been surprised to receive a call from Joey. He often complained about his neighbour. Usually they told him to go to sleep and phone back in the morning, but he rarely called back. This call was different, though. Joey repeated several times, "We got into a fight and I think I killed him." They phoned the rescue team and asked them to get over to Two Mile Island as soon as possible. It would take forty-five minutes to cross the half-frozen river from the mainland and it would be a hell of a job crossing. The phone rang again. Joey wanted to know why it was taking them so long.

Bill Jacobs and John Gabriel who were on rescue duty that evening both knew Joey. They sprang into action, and within moments were at the dock facing the island. The firemen who were called had devised a plan to cross the river using a rubber dinghy with long ropes, hooks, and pulleys. Jacobs and Gabriel would have to paddle through the icy water. When the trip was completed, a pulley would be attached to a tree on the island and the dinghy could be pulled back and forth between the island and the mainland.

The rescue team set off into the bitter cold. This had better be real or they would have some choice words for Joey. Even if he had killed a man, why couldn't he have chosen a warmer night? In the distance they saw a light in the house. They thought they'd caught a glimpse of a man down at the dock, but it must have been an illusion. Half an hour later, they arrived on the island, attached the pulley to the tree, and overturned the dinghy to protect it from the blowing snow. They raced up to the house. There was no path to the front door, so they walked around to the shed and entered the house. Joey was seated alone at the table drinking vodka. He gestured to a body on the floor in the corner of the living room and muttered, "Over there. Get that damn monkey out of here."

They moved towards the corner and swung Scattered Dust's limp body around so they could insert a tube in his mouth. Blood gushed all over the floor. There was no detectable pulse or heartbeat. The CPR course had not trained them to revive the dead. Yes, Joey had killed a man.

The Mohawk police on the mainland had given a radio instruction for one of them to return with the dinghy and the other to stay with Joey. The coroner and the provincial police would be called in, since the Mohawk police were not equipped or trained for murder investigations. Gabriel went down to the water and arranged for the return of the dinghy. Jacobs stayed in the house with Joey, who kept sipping vodka and repeating, "We had a fight and I killed him. Look at the bump on my head."

Joey didn't give the police any resistance. He seemed dazed when they read him his rights, though he nodded his head in feigned understanding. He repeated to them as he had to Jacobs, "We had a fight and I guess I killed him."

When asked how he did it, he led them to a cupboard underneath the steps and pointed to an old aluminum baseball bat that had bloodstains on it. The cupboard door was left open so the technician would not miss the bat.

Joey dressed in his jacket and toque and the police put handcuffs on his wrists. They crossed in the dinghy to the mainland, where a waiting patrol car took him to the police station. It was four o'clock in the morning. Later Joey was taken to the interview room. The policemen reminded him of the circumstances of his arrest and that he had been read his rights. They asked a few questions, and he responded by pointing to the top of his head. The police took Joey to the hospital where the doctor on duty in the emergency room examined his head. It was sensitive to the touch, but the doctor could see nothing seriously wrong, so he recommended Tylenol and cold compresses. The X-rays showed that Joey had previously had surgery on that part of his head. When the police took him back to town, Joey was arraigned and charged with the second-degree murder of Charlie "Scattered Dust" Morris.

"The Crown must prove the essential elements or ingredients of the offence. They most prove beyond a reasonable doubt that Joey Gordon was the person involved, the date and place, the identity of the victim, that the death resulted from an unlawful act of the accused, and that the accused meant to cause the death of the victim.

"I expect you will not have trouble satisfying yourselves as to the existence of most of these elements. However, the proof of intent may present some difficulty. Intention is the difference between murder and manslaughter. If the accused struck the victim with a baseball

bat, did he mean to cause death? Or was death a consequence of an illegal act devoid of intention to cause death? Before you decide that question, you should examine the defence. Joey Gordon pleads that he acted in self-defence to repel the unprovoked assault by Scattered Dust, that he feared he would suffer death or grievous bodily injury, and could not otherwise save himself. His only reasonable alternative was to strike Scattered Dust with the bat . . . "

This was the heart of the case. The pathologist had testified that death could have resulted from any one of the three fatal blows to the head of the victim. There were signs of other blows to the head, as well as eight blows to the body. Scattered Dust had been struck thirteen times with a hard blunt object. One or two of the wounds may have been caused by his fall.

The police officers described the arrest and visit to the hospital. Three policemen had seen the bump on Joey's head.

The rescue squad testified as well. They had done their best, but there was no chance of saving the victim. The blood on the bat and the blood on Joey's jeans matched the blood sample of the victim. The statements of the rescue squad and police officers were conclusive.

Joey had killed Scattered Dust, but why and in what circumstances. Who had started the brawl? What had really happened? Only two men knew, and one of them was dead. The other was entitled to remain silent. An accused is not obliged to testify.

The defence called Doctor Fred Morton as its first witness. Five years earlier, he had treated Joey for injuries from a blow to the head and removed a blood clot. The area around the wound remained sensitive and vulnerable.

There was a hush in the courtroom. Would the only living witness testify? Although Joey was entitled to remain silent and claim the benefit of doubt, juries like to hear the accused. Silence can be interpreted as an admission of guilt or cowardice and fear of cross-examination. The decision was announced:

Joey would testify. The courtroom suddenly filled as the guards accompanied him from the prisoner's dock to the witness box. I ordered his handcuffs removed. Joey spoke slowly and cautiously.

"We were sitting and drinking. I told Scattered Dust to leave, but he wouldn't. I phoned my brother to tell him to leave, but Robert wouldn't get involved. We talked of electricity. Then I went out to piss. When I came back, Scattered Dust was standing there with a baseball bat. He swung the bat at me and I ducked. He stood between me and the shed. The front door wouldn't open. The manure was blocking the door and it was frozen. I was scared like hell. You know I got a hole in my head and it still hurts from the time before when I was hit in the head. I knew if he hit me one, it would be goodbye Joey. The second time he swung the bat, I grabbed it with my hand. The bat hit the side of my head, where I have a bump. At the same time, I punched his face. I used to be a boxer. I went down on my knees. We struggled for the bat, then I got it loose and swung at his legs and body over and over again. Once I hit his head and he fell. He didn't get up. I saw blood on the floor and on my jeans. I didn't know he was dead and was afraid he would start again. I hid the bat in the cupboard so he wouldn't find it. Then I called the police. He could have killed me. I didn't have to give him electricity. It costs a lot in the winter . . . ."

I glanced at the men and women on the jury, grateful that they and not I would have to decide the guilt or innocence of the accused.

"It has been said that the judge is the master of the law. Well, not quite, the law is the master of the judge. Just as the law is my master, the evidence presented in this courtroom is your master. Did the evidence convince you beyond a reasonable doubt that the plea of self-defence is unfounded? Who started the fight? If Joey did not have a reasonable fear of death from the assault by the victim, it is your duty to find him guilty. If Joey knew he could escape harm by

other means than striking Scattered Dust, it is your duty to find him guilty. But if there remains a reasonable doubt in your mind as to these matters, you must accept the plea of self-defence and find the accused 'not guilty.' You should now retire and consider your verdict . . . "

The jury deliberated for five hours. They obtained and reheard the tapes of Joey's testimony. At six o'clock the jurors went for dinner at the Old Spaghetti House. Fifteen minutes after they returned, I was sent a note that they were ready to give their verdict. As a wedding gift, juror number five was chosen to announce the verdict. They found Joey not guilty. I accepted the verdict and ordered his immediate release.

Two Mile Island lies three hundred yards from the mainland. It is part of an Indian reserve. There are two homes on the island but only one is occupied. A man lives alone there. His name is Joey Gordon. He is rarely seen. The kids fear him and no longer play baseball on the island in the summer. They say he killed a man . . .

13
The Robbery

Mickey Brown had been a jeweller all his life. He'd learned the trade from his father. He could tell the difference between a real diamond and a fake one at a glance; a simple touch was sufficient for him to distinguish an eighteen-carat gold chain from a ten-carat one. Although he had never managed to break into the big leagues, he was proud of his small store on St. Catherine Street. On a good Saturday, he would sell several thousand dollars of watches, bangles, and trinkets to the "street people" as he called the passersby.

Then, of course, there were the "home people." They were the home owners who were referred to him by satisfied customers. Mickey would receive them in the small private office at the rear of the store and invite them to choose from the collection of fine jewellery and precious stones that he kept in the safe. The street people paid the rent and the overhead, but the home people contributed the money for his luxuries.

The duplex in Montreal's respectable Notre Dame de

Grâce neighbourhood, the car his son drove to college, the condo in Hallandale, Florida — they were all purchased with money earned from the home people. The old Chevrolet, the food on his family's table, the insurance and taxes on his house, these were paid with profits from the street people. He made a good living and even had a little left over to pay taxes.

Mickey spent most of his time in the jewellery store. It was open daily from ten o'clock in the morning till six in the evening. On Fridays, the store stayed open till nine, but Mickey had resisted the move to remain open on Thursday evenings. A man had to have time for his family.

Mickey didn't work alone. He employed a saleswoman to help with the street people and take messages when he was out. After all, a small businessman had to get out to visit suppliers and scout the competition. At least once a week, Mickey would walk west along St. Catherine Street as far as Guy Street and look into the windows of every jewellery store. He even visited the jewellery counters in the department stores. The market survey would invariably end with a leisurely stroll through Henry Birks & Sons, the largest and best-known jeweller in Montreal. He boasted that his prices were half those charged by Birks.

"Tell me what you'd pay at Birks and I'll sell it to you for half price," he would tell the home people.

And, "At Birks, you buy overhead, at Mickey's you buy merchandise."

Mickey would utter these stirring phrases two or three times daily.

On Monday, dealers' day, he visited the small manufacturers and jobbers who supplied him with stock. His itinerary took him to three or four factories and several importers and jobbers, where he looked for last year's rings, bracelets, and chains that were being cleared at bargain prices, and precious stones with barely perceptible flaws that were being sold below market prices. In this way, he kept his store full and managed to undersell Birks.

Back at his place of business, Mickey watched the people walk along St. Catherine Street. He could separate the buyers from the lookers just as surely as he could separate glass beads from diamonds. Each time the front door opened, he knew instinctively if the intruder was a buyer or a looker, a street person or a home person.

Street people were left to Isabelle because she knew how to speak to them. She would show thirty-five rings to a looker, never betraying a hint of impatience. Occasionally, a looker would buy a ring or a bracelet and Isabelle would chide Mickey for his mistaken assessment.

"You never can tell. Today's looker is tomorrow's buyer," she would say with a smile.

"Not with street people," he would reply. "Home people, yes. Today they look, tonight they sleep with their husbands, and tomorrow they buy. But street people? Once a looker, always a looker. When a looker becomes a buyer it's because they have a poor memory and forgot that they're lookers and not buyers."

During the slow season, which lasted about nine months of the year, he would make these simple philosophical statements to Isabelle, read the newspapers and catalogues, and watch the endless parade of people on the street. During the busy season — that is, in the months of May, November, and December — he would be preoccupied with the customers.

Mickey would never forget the day of the robbery. He had been sitting in the office reading his newspaper when a looker entered the store. He dismissed the young man with a glance and kept studying the newsprint. Isabelle could handle the situation. She removed the small trays of gold chains from the showcase and showed them to the customer one at a time. Each chain was lifted and displayed against the velvet cushion. When the customer showed interest, she would place the chain over her arm or around her neck.

Suddenly, the man reached down into his pocket and took out a small pistol. He ordered Isabelle to lie down on the floor behind the counter. Mickey came alive and instinctively pushed the alarm button under his desktop. He knew from experience that the police would appear within five minutes. There was no point in trying to be a hero. The young man pointed the pistol at Mickey, ordered him to come out of the office and lie down beside Isabelle on the floor behind the back counter. Then in a simple motion, he tipped the counter on top of them. As the contents of the counter spilled to the floor, the robber pulled a green plastic bag from his pocket, filled it with handfuls of watches, rings, and chains, and ran from the store. The entire robbery had taken less than one minute.

Mickey pushed the counter upright as he struggled to his feet. Then he ran to lock the front door.

"Don't touch anything," he ordered Isabelle. "The police will be here in a minute. Remember what he looked like. Try to remember all the details. Don't touch anything until the police have seen the mess."

"M-m-m-Mickey," she stammered, "he pointed his gun at me. I could have been killed."

"He didn't fire, and you were very brave. Stay calm. Look, the police are here," Mickey said, as he opened the locked door.

The police were thorough and efficient. One officer made a sketch of the store. His partner took statements from Mickey and Isabelle and phoned the description of the robber to the station. This was the third such robbery that day and they were convinced the criminal would slip up and be caught soon. They thanked Mickey for his cooperation, promised to inform him of developments and asked him to send a full list of the stolen jewellery so they could complete their report.

As they left, Mickey locked the door behind them and hung a Closed sign in the window. He told Isabelle to take the rest of the day off and gave her a twenty-dollar bill.

"Here, it's been a rough day. Go home and take your husband out for dinner on me. It will help you forget. But don't forget too much. I still have to deal with the insurance company and you are the eyewitness. Go home and take it easy."

"Thanks," replied Isabelle, as she took her sweater off the hanger in the rear office, grimaced at Mickey, and left.

He locked the door once again and returned to the office. First he called his wife to describe the day's events, then he called his insurance agent to report the loss. This was not his first robbery, and he knew the routine. Mickey insisted that the agent report to the insurance company and have them send an adjustor immediately. He would stay in the store to receive the adjustor and show him the mess that afternoon. Naturally, it would take him a week or so to prepare a proper inventory and calculate the loss.

Late that afternoon, the adjustor arrived and identified himself to Mickey by showing his business card through the door window.

Mark Lapointe
Expert en sinistres — Insurance adjustor
J.P. Dennis Inc.

The adjustor photographed the interior of the store, questioned Mickey, and promised to return the following week. He gave Mickey authorization to clean up the mess and requested that the written claim be sent to him for processing. The insurers would insist that the past five years of Mickey's book be audited by their accountants.

Mickey listened intently. He had anticipated everything except the five-year audit. That might be a small problem, because his bookkeeper was not a chartered accountant. Mickey would hire a real accountant to write up the books. The accountant would be a valuable witness anyway, if the claim ever went to court. Mickey decided to make a large claim, of at least $30,000.

The insurers denied liability on the grounds that Mickey had failed to respect the condition of the policy, which obliged him to keep a perpetual inventory and complete and accurate books and records in which all purchases and sales were accurately recorded. Mickey hired a lawyer and sued his insurers. Twenty-three months after the robbery, the trial began before me.

The presentation of Mickey's evidence was straightforward. Isabelle Morin was an excellent witness. She spoke of her years in Mickey's employ, the good relationship they enjoyed, and how respectfully she was treated. She described the robbery in vivid detail. Listening to her, I could easily visualize the entire episode in the jewellery shop from the moment the robber entered until his hasty departure. I did not for a moment doubt the accuracy of her testimony. The police officers confirmed that they had arrived at the shop after receiving notice of the alarm, and they confirmed Isabelle's recital of the morning's events.

Mickey's version of the robbery dovetailed neatly with those of the other witnesses, and he held up well during cross-examination on the details of his bookkeeping practices. The inventory control system was primitive but probably adequate to meet the requirements of the insurance policy. When questioned about sales that may not have been recorded in his books, Mickey stared straight at me, and in a low, steady voice, denied the possibility of any unrecorded sales of jewellery. Perhaps the sale of a watch strap or occasional repair was accidentally omitted, but that would have been pure oversight.

The final witness, the accountant, stated that he had been

engaged after the robbery to verify the books and records and had performed all the usual checks, and in his opinion, the books were complete and accurate, reflected all income and expenses, and complied fully with the requirements of the insurance policy. He considered the inventory control system to be simple but adequate. Mickey listened to this testimony with an air of deep concentration. These accountants were expensive, but they were worth every cent. When the accountant's cross-examination was concluded, Mickey's attorney announced that the plaintiff's proof was closed.

The insurers recalled the investigating police officer as their first witness. He described how he had received the radio call from the dispatcher and proceeded immediately to the jewellery store, "I arrived on the scene with my partner. He stayed in the lane beside the store while I entered. Can I consult my . . . "

At that moment a disembodied voice called from the speaker phone in front of the court clerk: "Attention all security personnel. This is a ten thirteen. I repeat, attention all security personnel, this is a ten thirteen."

Mickey's attorney rose and addressed me: "My lord, this must be a serious matter. Should we leave the building?"

"I don't think that will be necessary. All I heard was numbers called to the courthouse security personnel. If it's necessary for us to leave, I am sure they will say so in unambiguous terms."

"May I ask the police officer a question?"

"Yes," I replied.

"Officer," he asked, "do you know what a ten thirteen is?"

"No, it must be an internal security code."

I glanced at the clock and noted that it was a quarter to twelve. Whatever the explanation of the ten thirteen, it was obvious that the attorneys and the witnesses were upset. I looked from one attorney to the next and asked, "Gentlemen, would you prefer to adjourn now and resume at two o'clock in the afternoon?"

"Yes, my lord," they answered in unison.

"Fine, the Court will adjourn until two o'clock. If you experience difficulty re-entering the building, wait until three and call my office for information. Should the problems continue beyond three o'clock, you can assume that the hearing is continued to nine-thirty tomorrow morning. Since we are on the second floor, I suggest that you use the stairs to leave. The elevators may be crowded or closed. The Court is adjourned."

The lawyers and witnesses departed rapidly. Turning to Linda, I remarked, "Let's go up and see what's happening. I hope the elevators are still running. Otherwise I'll have to leave the building. You know the routine. Once you go out, the guards won't let you come in until the ten thirteen is over."

The judges' elevator functioned normally and I made it back to my office. Jackie looked at me quizzically and asked, "Is your case finished? I expected you to be gone for the day."

"No, it's not finished. Your friends downstairs have been shouting numbers into my courtroom."

"What numbers? We didn't hear anything in the office."

"Ten thirteen, I think. Did you say there was no disruption or announcement in the offices?"

"Not a word, and I would know. I'm responsible for security on the north side of the fifteenth floor."

"I know. I know. Why don't you call Rocket and ask him what's happening? Better still, invite him to drop by for a cup of coffee at my expense. Tell him we only want information and will not make any demands on his budget."

"I shall call immediately, but I cannot understand why the announcement was made on your floor only. Where did you say you were sitting?"

"On the second floor. One room was unoccupied and they assigned it to me."

"But, *Monsieur le juge*," she continued, "that explains why I didn't know. You were sitting in zone two and our office is in zone seven. Zone two is the busiest area in the building. That explains everything. It was a zone two emergency."

"Jackie," I said, "that explains nothing. Call Rocket and tell him to fly up and see me. His ten thirteen will probably cost me half a day."

Jackie made a face as she picked up the phone.

"Hello, hello, Monsieur Racine . . . "

Fifteen minutes later Rocket Racine entered my office. Jackie followed, carrying a tray with three cups of coffee. I motioned to the chairs and said, "Sit down, please, sit down."

Jackie gave us each a cup of coffee. I smiled at Rocket and asked, "How are things at the Maintenance these days?"

"Very difficult, very difficult," he replied. "Once again the treasury board has ordered that we cut back our budgets. It will be a year of shortages. I had intended to change the carpets on this floor, but alas . . . " he looked at the ceiling and lifted both arms.

"Monsieur Racine," I said, "I do not wish to ask an indiscreet question, but would you happen to know why there was a ten thirteen — ?"

"In zone two," my secretary interjected.

"*Monsieur le juge*, the investigation is not complete, but I can assure you that there is no danger. The security guards have informed me what happened. Of course, this is verbal and subject to written confirmation. A report will be filed at our meeting this Friday."

"If you tell me what happened, I shall keep it in the strictest confidence," I assured him.

"And," said Jackie, "I am a member of the security team. I am the floor warden for the fifteenth floor north."

Rocket bent forward and lowered his voice.

"*Monsieur le juge*, one of your colleagues was presiding in practice court on the second floor, which is in zone two. In those courtrooms, a judge hears many applications in a day and there is a constant hum of conversation. Lawyers enter and leave continually. During a lapse in the hearings, an intermittent beep was heard. The room became silent and all eyes turned towards a briefcase on the floor in the rear corner of the courtroom. The judge asked if anyone in the room owned the briefcase. When no one responded, he ordered everyone to leave until further notice and instructed his clerk to call security. We called an immediate zone two ten thirteen. In the meantime, the bomb squad entered the room and dismantled the briefcase on the floor where the beeps originated. They discovered that someone had failed to shut off a small dictation machine and the intermittent beeps signalled that the tape was at an end."

"Hubert," I said, "I shall continue my case this afternoon secure in the knowledge that we are protected by palace security. I appreciate your coming here and wish you success with your cutbacks. *Au revoir*."

"*Au revoir, Monsieur le juge.* Good rest of the day, Madame Jackie."

When the trial resumed I informed the parties that my inquiries confirmed there was no danger and we were in the safe and secure hands of the palace security.

The testimony of the police officer was rapidly completed and the defence called Mark Lapointe as their next witness.

He outlined his professional experience, described the investigation, including his visit to the store on the day of the robbery, his interviews with Mickey and Isabelle, and his calls upon several of Mickey's suppliers and a few of his customers. He mentioned that two of Mickey's customers had been unable to produce bills for jewellery they had purchased and claimed they had lost them.

The final witness for the insurers was Benoit Caron, chartered accountant, and managing partner of Gendron, Robert, Caron. He was a former officer of the Institute of Chartered Accountants, a professor at Concordia University, and an expert in bankruptcy investigations with particular experience in the field of jewellery theft. He was the partner in charge of the audit of four substantial retail jewellers, several watch importers, and half a dozen manufacturers of rings, bracelets, and chains.

Caron described the elaborate perpetual inventory records maintained by all of his retail clients. Most used computerized systems; in his opinion Mickey's manual system was archaic and inaccurate. He produced a series of large spread sheets, which were filed as exhibits, and presented a detailed analysis of Mickey's financial statements for the previous five years. Caron analyzed various ratios and profit margins, and elaborated on substantial variations from year to year, which he described as "gyrations." The magnitude of the fluctuations in these ratios, he said, rendered the financial statements untrustworthy.

He concluded that the statements must contain substantial omissions, and undoubtedly Mickey was conducting a large volume of business that was not recorded in the books of his business. This failure to record sales made it impossible to reconstruct the inventory and determine the amount of the loss. In brief, although the robbery could not be denied, in his opinion, no accountant could certify the amount of the loss. Moreover, this was a flagrant violation of the condition inserted in the policy that would allow the insurers to verify losses in cases of this nature.

As I listened to Benoit Caron's testimony and followed his analysis of Mickey's statements, it became readily apparent to me that Mickey had lied. His accounting records were incomplete. There was no other rational explanation for the year-to-year fluctuations in the profit margins.

Mickey had failed to respect an essential condition of the insurance policy and this would be fatal to his claim. Even if I held that the policy remained in effect, he could not satisfy me as to the amount of his loss. There could be no doubt that the store had been robbed in broad daylight. Isabelle Morin had told the complete truth, but I would have to dismiss Mickey's action.

My problem was not what to decide, but how to explain my decision in simple, clear terms, so obvious that even Mickey would be unable to question the logic of the decision. The conclusion of a judgment is for the benefit of the winner, the reasons for judgment provide an explanation to the loser. He may not always agree with the judgment, but I consider it a personal challenge to convince the unsuccessful party that I heard and understood his arguments, even if I did not agree with them. That is why I usually deliver my judgment in open court at the conclusion of the trial, rather than drafting a written judgment that is mailed to the lawyers and parties several months later. As I render the judgment, I look at the losing party and his attorney for a signal of understanding. If I fail, then I, as an individual, have fallen short of their and my expectations. The loser is the victim of my shortcomings and not of some impersonal, inhuman system.

Mickey would have trouble accepting a decision based on Caron's financial analysis and comparisons. It's hard to decide that a man's books and records are inaccurate because of gyrating ratios and profit margins. There had to be something simpler and more obvious.

I took Mickey's financial statements home that night. They had been signed by Mickey, and the logic of my judgment had to be grounded in his signed statements and not based solely on Caron's testimony. I read and reread those statements a dozen times. Not a single figure or note attracted my attention. And then I realized that the trial was not about what was recorded in the books but about what was not recorded.

215

Mickey was accused by his insurers of not recording sales. I would not find the unrecorded sales. But what of the expenses? I scanned the expenses once again, looking for obvious omissions. The answer jumped out. Mickey's statements did not show an expense for salaries. There could be no doubt that Isabelle Morin was an employee. She received a salary, or should have, but there was no mention of her salary in the statements of the business. She must have been paid in cash out of the money generated from unrecorded sales.

This could not be an oversight. If her salary of $15,000 or $20,000 a year was not recorded in the books of the business, there must be unrecorded sales of an equivalent amount and probably much more.

The attorneys completed their closing arguments the following morning. I waited a few minutes, arranged and re-arranged my notes, and then began to recite the judgment. Mickey looked at me intently while I read a paragraph from the insurance policy, described the events which gave rise to the claim, and analyzed the testimony of the witnesses. Mickey's face darkened when I summarized the financial analysis and conclusions of Benoit Caron and I declared that Benoit Caron's opinion about unrecorded sales was corroborated by the existence of unrecorded expenses such as the salary of Isabelle Morin, who was undoubtedly paid in cash out of the proceeds of unrecorded sales. For a brief moment I saw Mickey's head move up and down and his eyes close unconsciously.

"For the foregoing reasons, the plaintiff's action is dismissed with costs."

I rose and left the courtroom.

Mickey had been the victim of a robbery and had suffered a real loss. He was not reimbursed by his insurers. He was penalized for his failure to respect the terms of the insurance policy. Neither he, the insurers, nor I would ever know the true amount of the loss. The judgment was correct in law and was not appealed, but I have a lingering feeling that the best result may not have been achieved. Mickey's loss may have been disproportionate to his fault.

14
A Hedge

Laval de Coster stood on a stepladder squinting at the sun and enjoying the sound of his electric hedge trimmer. He was proud of the cedar hedge surrounding his property and looked forward to Sunday mornings in the late spring when he could trim and admire it. He glanced at the For Sale sign at the corner of his property, scowled, and then returned to his work. Laval was a self-made man who took particular pride in his achievements. His parents had given him an impressive-sounding name and little else. Occasionally, when dealing with lawyers and accountants, he felt upstaged, but after all, he was the one who managed the apartment buildings and the shopping centre, and they were paid to do his bidding. Not bad for a fellow who hadn't gone to college.

He had a nice home, but it seemed small now that his boys were getting older, and he wanted to find something closer to the centre of town. The boys would appreciate it. They shouldn't have to travel for an hour to get to university. George, the eldest, would be at University of Montreal in September. The house was small, but the grounds and cedar hedge were magnificent. If only he could find a similar property in Outremont, close to the university.

Tony Verdi emerged from the house on the other side of the hedge. What the hell did he want? Laval didn't know and quite frankly didn't care. He pretended not to notice his approaching neighbour and concentrated on his work. Verdi persisted. He walked right up to the hedge, stood under the hedge trimmer, waved his hands, and shouted.

"Hey, hey, good morning up there. I must speak to you."

There was no avoiding him. Laval flipped the switch and the noise of the trimmer stopped.

"Good morning," he answered without enthusiasm. "What do you want?"

"The hedge," said Tony, "there is something wrong with the hedge. I checked my deeds and I am missing some land. I want to install a heat pump and I do not have the space near my house. I checked the deeds twice. I should have eight feet between my house and the boundary and there are only three feet. The hedge must be in the wrong place."

"What are you talking about?" asked Laval. "This hedge must be as old as our homes and was planted on the property line. If there's a problem, I can come over on your side and trim a few inches. It's always wider in the spring."

"That would not be enough. I'm missing five feet of my property. I intend to call a surveyor and measure the property. Will you pay half the fee?"

"I won't pay half of anything. The hedge is on the property line and you're wasting your money. You should pay me for keeping the hedge so beautiful. You get a free view from the side windows of your house."

"I'm getting a surveyor," said Tony as he turned away. Looking back for a moment, he added, "And if the hedge is in the wrong place, it will be removed."

Laval's morning had been spoiled by the intrusion. "You touch one branch without my approval, and my fist will have to be removed . . . from your nose," he shouted. Laval tried to go on manicuring the hedge, but he had lost his enthusiasm. He put the hedge trimmer down and decided to finish the job later in the day.

He walked around to the back of the house. Why had the Majors sold their home to those wretched people? He had never had problems with the Majors. True, they had also tried to claim the hedge was on their property, and they had even offered to sell him a piece of their land for $5,000, but he had made a counter-offer of $1,000 and the conversation had ended. The Majors had never suggested that he remove the hedge, though. They knew how much pleasure and value a hedge could add to a property. They trimmed their side, and each year complimented him on the hedge's vigorous growth and colour. They had even offered to pay half the cost of the "cedar feeder" that he used for fertilizer. Now *they* were neighbours; the new people were just intruders. But the whole thing would soon be over anyway. After all, his house was for sale, the market was strong, and the new owners could squabble with the Verdis.

There was no point in getting all upset for nothing. Laval reminded himself that he was a fortunate man. He had a beautiful, lively wife, Marika, and fine sons, and he had made his mark in the real estate community. Satisfied, he forgot about Tony Verdi.

Several weeks passed. Laval was at the office and Marika was sitting at the kitchen table enjoying a lazy second cup of coffee when she heard the roar of a chainsaw outside. She walked over to the kitchen window, looked out, and saw two men cutting down her hedge. Marika picked up the phone and dialed 911.

"Please, send the police. Someone is destroying the hedge on my property," she shouted. Then she tightened the belt on her bathrobe and rushed out to confront the workmen. She ran around the end of the hedge, stood beside the men, and shouted, "Stop, stop, what are you doing?" Her shouts were drowned out by the blaring noise of the chainsaw.

"Stop, stop!" she pleaded. "Stop those saws!" They continued unmoved.

Marika knew the police would come in a minute. The question was how to delay the destruction of her hedge until they arrived. She grabbed a rake that was leaning against the side of her house and tried to poke it through the hedge where the men were working. Her efforts were futile. The cedar shrubs just kept falling before the saw. Then she remembered the hose. She ran to the corner of the house, turned on the hose, and began spraying the men with water, but they kept on going. So she ran around the hedge and tried to protect the shrubs with her body.

At that moment a cruiser pulled up in front of the house. Marika ran up to greet them, shouting, "They're cutting my hedge. They're destroying my property. Stop them! Stop them!"

With a wave of his hand the police officer managed to accomplish what Marika had been unable to do with the rake and the hose. The noise stopped; there was an ominous silence.

"What is going on here?" inquired the officer.

"They're destroying my hedge! They're cutting my cedars! Who are they? Who sent them?" she shouted.

"Calm down, Madam," said the officer. He walked over to the older of the workmen.

"Who engaged you and what exactly are you doing?"

The man stepped forward. "We are cutting the hedge on Mr. Verdi's property. We have a contract to cut it. He said we might have some trouble, but I never expected that this madwoman would try to hit us with her rake and act like she was out of her mind. These are cedar shrubs. We're not killing anyone. Would you like to see our contract?"

"Yes," said the police officer as he and the workman walked

towards the truck together. The two men looked at some papers for a minute, brought them back, and handed them over to the police officer. "They have a contract to cut the hedge," he said to Marika after looking at the documents, "and they even have a survey plan showing that the hedge is on the property of your neighbour, Mr. Verdi. There is nothing we can do. This is a civil matter and they are acting within their rights."

Marika stared at the police officer in disbelief. She muttered, "I called you and you say there is nothing you can do, nothing you can do, a civil matter. Those trees are mine, they are living trees, and you say there is nothing you can do?"

At that moment, the workman started up his chainsaw again. Marika ran forward to shield the trees with her body. This time the police officers grabbed her by the arms and forced her into the back of their car. She shivered, sobbed, and resisted without success. From the back of the cruiser she watched the cedar hedge disappear. It was all over in fifteen minutes. The hedge had been cut. All that remained were stumps and roots. Marika kept weeping and shivering.

"Calm down, Madam," said the police officer. "There will not be any more cutting of the hedge. We will take you into the house and you should relax. Take a cup of coffee."

Her strength was gone. She meekly stepped from the car and allowed herself to be led from the car to the sidewalk, up the stairs, and into the house. The police officer lingered a minute until he saw her seated in the den, next to the phone. He bowed slowly and left, muttering under his breath.

"Goodbye, Madam. Goodbye, Madam."

Marika lifted the phone slowly and called Laval's office. When she heard his voice, she sobbed, "They cut the hedge, they cut the hedge, they cut the hedge . . . "

Laval didn't need further details. He ran from his office, got into his car, and raced up the expressway. Half an hour later when he arrived in front of the house, he could see at a glance that the hedge he had nurtured over the years was gone. There was only emptiness between his home and the damn Verdis. The workmen were removing the remaining stumps and roots. They had tied one end of a rope to the bumper of their truck and fastened the other end to several of the stumps. On a signal, the driver of the truck would gun the motor, and as the truck jumped forward, the stumps of the cedars were wrenched from the ground.

Laval drove his car over the sidewalk and parked on his lawn parallel to the street. Perhaps his parked car would somehow slow down or impede the removal of the stumps. He bounded up the stairs into the house and found Marika seated by the telephone, staring blankly and repeating, "They cut the hedge. The police helped them cut the hedge. They cut the hedge. . . ." She stopped, choked back a few sobs, and then continued, "They cut the hedge, they cut the hedge. . . ."

He placed his arms around his wife and pulled her body towards him. She did not resist. She just lay limply in his arms, sobbing and muttering in a low voice, "They cut the hedge, they cut the hedge . . . " Laval led Marika to their bedroom. He gave her a sleeping pill and stayed by her side while she sobbed herself to sleep. He then went down the stairs, took a pencil and paper from the phone table, walked outside, and slowly wrote down the name and address on the truck door. He returned to the house and stared defiantly at the space where his hedge had once stood. He would fight, but not today. Today he had Marika to worry about. But he would make those Verdis regret they'd ever been born. And those gardeners or whatever the hell the workmen were, he would sue them for every last cent. He had lawyers. They would make those gardeners sorry they'd ever come to his street. Verdi would pay dearly.

Marika didn't recover from the trauma. She took more sleeping pills and slept less. She was constantly tired and neglected her household duties. Her weight dropped, her clothes hung loosely on her body, and the sparkle left her blue eyes. She would no longer leave the house and remained indoors for days at a time. She even rejected her husband's night-time overtures. Afraid to sleep, she would lie in bed with her eyes open. The moment she closed her eyes, she could hear the chainsaw and feel the police officers force her into the back seat of their car where she was a silent witness to the nightly destruction of the hedge.

Laval thought her condition would improve with time, but it didn't. He took her to see doctors, psychologists, and psychiatrists. They were unable to help. The insomnia, the pills, and the nightmares continued. He dreaded to come home at night. He could not bear to see her suffering. Even the boys seemed to find new and more original excuses to stay at school or sleep over at the homes of their friends.

Laval consulted his lawyers. They examined the title deeds, ordered still another survey of the property and informed Laval that he had no case. The cedar shrubs had been planted on the neighbour's property and he was entitled to cut them. Laval refused to accept their opinion.

"What are you lawyers good for? Anyone can make a lease or go to the rental board. Go look in those damn books of yours and find a law, find a way to make Verdi pay. If you can't, I'll get lawyers who can."

Once again his attorneys studied the law, and this time they developed a strategy to claim ownership of the land where the hedge stood. They discovered a law that imposes a penalty, albeit a modest one, for the illegal cutting of trees. They engaged landscape architects to establish a value for the replacement of the shrubs and instituted an action. They claimed $75,000 in damages for the cost of replacing the lost shrubs, the decreased value of the home, and the personal suffering and anguish of Marika, and a fine of $1.50 for each shrub that was cut.

Verdi counterclaimed, requesting that the de Costers be ordered to remove several feet of stone wall along the front of the property which according to the survey also encroached on his property. He also arranged for the erection of a grey metal chainlink fence, six feet high, along the boundary of his property. Good fences make good neighbours.

Thirty-four months after the cutting of the hedge, the trial began before me. I had read the written proceedings, seen the pictures of the hedge and the chainlink fence that replaced it, and examined the medical reports on Marika's health. It all seemed curiously unreal. The file looked like a tempest in a teapot, a neighbourly squabble over a few shrubs. It didn't make sense. The procedures must contain exaggerated claims and absurd conjecture.

Marika attended the trial. She was dressed in black and sat passively beside her attorney. The facts were presented dispassionately. The surveyors, the policemen, the gardeners, Laval de Coster, Tony Verdi, and the landscape architect all testified.

The second day began with the medical testimony. The psychiatrist explained how Marika had been referred by one of his former students. She was addicted to drugs, anorexic, suffering from insomnia and agoraphobia, and was generally depressed. He had done his best and had managed to wean her from the stronger drugs onto weaker ones. In the midst of his testimony, he suddenly said, "*Monsieur le juge*, you would not have reacted so violently nor would I have, but make no mistake about it. The condition of this woman, the disintegration of her life, was directly attributable to her experience that day, when the hedge was cut."

I listened to his words and believed his testimony. I was an involuntary witness to the inadequacy of the law. I could not help Marika or even order that she be compensated for the loss of her shrubs. Tony Verdi had cut shrubs on his property and he was entitled to do so. He was entitled to prefer a grey metal chainlink fence to an eight-foot vibrant living cedar hedge. The action by the de Costers was dismissed.

Laval de Coster may have been a self-made man whose name was known in the real estate industry, but he made the mistake of not buying a few feet of land when they were offered to him and he made the mistake of not discussing the hedge with Tony Verdi. Small errors that cast a long shadow. I could find no remedy in law for Marika.

15

Visits

Gerry Rousseau lay on his bed staring at the ceiling. Tomorrow he would be allowed to leave the grounds of the Lepine Institute and visit Corinne. Two years had elapsed since the accident. That was a long time to be locked up in a mental hospital. He frowned for a moment and then a smile returned to his lips. Two years was also a long time for a man to sleep alone, but tomorrow . . . tomorrow he would visit Corinne. He longed for the closeness of his woman. Despite two years of separation, he could remember every line and curve of her body. Corinne did not abandon him after the accident. At first she could not visit often because Nancy was only an infant and it was hard to travel with her. During the past year, however, they had visited him more frequently.

Nancy was his daughter, a bright, inquisitive, and friendly child who was constantly talking and making noises. Her big blue eyes and dark hair were just like her mother's. Nancy had been born just three days before the accident.

The doctor realized it was important for Gerry to attend Nancy's second birthday party and that is how he had managed to get a one-day pass. One day was not a long time compared with two years, but at least it was a start. And afterwards, he would be alone with Corinne. It would be good; everything would be good.

Some day he would have to tell Nancy about the accident. She must wonder why her father lived in a hospital and not at home like other fathers. Well, tomorrow he would live at home with Nancy and Corinne like a normal father. He would have to return at night, but some day he might be permitted to leave the Institute and never return.

Gerry closed his eyes briefly but was too excited to sleep. He looked around the sparsely furnished room. The furniture was merely adequate: a grey metal dresser with three drawers, two matching chairs, a small wooden table, a night table, and of course, the bed. He did not own many things — only his clothing and the small portable television set Corinne had given him last year. If he ever got out of the Institute he would buy more things. You couldn't buy much with the small salary he earned in the Maintenance Department.

They did trust him there. Gerry even had his own toolbox and was called whenever a plumbing repair was required. The $125 monthly salary wasn't a lot of money, but he gave Corinne $25 a month for the baby and could buy them the occasional small gift. Most of his salary was spent on cigarettes and chocolates. During his time at Lepine, he had managed to save $73, which he planned to use to buy a toy for Nancy and a bottle of perfume for Corinne.

Gerry and Corinne had met in high school when they were teenagers. They quit school at the same time and just drifted together. Neither of them had a regular job, but they managed to earn enough money to pay for their two-room basement apartment, some food, and a joint or two. When they couldn't find work, there was always unemployment insurance. As long as you worked some of the time, the government would support you the rest of the time. They knew how to work the system so there would always be some money coming into the house.

Corinne's pregnancy frightened and transformed him. Gerry did not want his child to be brought up in a home where the necessities were in short supply. He knew, first-hand, what it was like to have less than the other children in the area and feared he could not provide the baby with food, clothes, and toys. He blamed Corinne for the decision to have a child and they fought more frequently. Gerry would stomp out of the house, wander down to Dunkin' Donuts, an amusement arcade, or a bar to meet his friends and buy a joint or two. When all the money in his pocket was gone, he returned home, frustrated and depressed.

When Corinne went into labour Gerry wanted to go to the hospital, but instead he panicked and went searching for his friends, hoping that one of them would have an idea how he could make a fast buck. The child would need so much. At the bar he bumped into "Kid" Trent and sat beside him. Trent meant trouble, big trouble. He was a professional boxer who did most of his fighting in local bars and lived from one brawl to the next. Gerry and Kid drank together, exchanging few words. When he got back home, all Gerry could remember were Kid's final words: "Make damn sure you're there, or I'll break your back." He could not for the life of him recollect where he had promised to be or even when, but Kid's words reverberated in his head, "Make damn sure you're there, or I'll break your back."

The ringing telephone startled him. Corinne had called to announce that he was the father of a little girl, and the least he could do was get over to the hospital the next morning.

Two days later Corinne and the baby were discharged from the hospital and Gerry brought them home in a borrowed car. He was obsessed by the thought that since he had betrayed Kid, the boxer would show up at the apartment and harm Corinne or the baby. There was no choice but to run and hide. Corinne, however, was not impressed by his fears or his plans.

"You've been running ever since I got pregnant," she said with a shrug.

"No," he replied, "This is different. Before, I ran away to avoid facing you and the baby. Now I'm running to protect you. Lend me $40, please. I'll call you when I'm safe."

"You'll never be safe. If you're so afraid of Trent, why the hell don't you call the police? He's probably in jail. Take the money in the jar near the stove and go. We'll manage just fine without you. We'll get by with the money from the government. Just go away."

Gerry went into the kitchen and took the money from the jar. Then he returned to the bedroom, took a rifle out from under the bed, and left without turning back. Corinne wept softly.

For three hours, Gerry wandered through lanes and back alleys in the neighbourhood, trying desperately to keep out of sight until nightfall. He had no idea what to do after dark, but somehow it seemed he would be safer then. What had Corinne said? She had told him to call the police. Calling the police was not his style, but perhaps she was right. Maybe Kid *was* in jail and maybe he didn't remember anything about the meeting in the bar either. Well, no crime had been committed. Gerry searched in his pocket for a quarter. He had the $40 but no change. Besides, how could he walk into a convenience store carrying a rifle, ask for change to use the phone, and call the police. Some nervous cashier would press the alarm button and he would be in big trouble. But to leave the rifle on the street leaning against the building would be plain stupid. He would go to a private home, ask permission to use the phone, and hope they didn't panic at the sight of his rifle. Even better, he would conceal the rifle behind the shrubs in front of the house while he made his call.

He walked up the front steps of a small brick house on the

corner. A woman answered but refused to allow him in. She told him to wait while she called the police. Gerry did not argue. He just thanked her, went down the front stairs, and hid behind the shrubs in front of the building. As he crouched, clutching his rifle and waiting, Gerry began to think about Kid Trent. What if the woman knew Kid? Would she betray him? Sweat trickled down his trembling forehead. In the distance, a car turned the corner and drove down the street slowly and silently. Gerry stood and fired three shots as it approached. The brakes squealed, the siren wailed, and the car sped off. Through the passenger window he caught a glimpse of a blonde woman pitching forward. The noise of the brakes, tires, and siren magnified and echoed in his head. He dropped the rifle and covered his ears and then his eyes. The shot fired on the police car must have hit the blonde woman. What had he done?

The noise of the siren receded. Then it was joined by others as police cars converged upon the small brick house. Terrified by the lights and shouts, Gerry staggered out, his arms raised. Within seconds, he was surrounded by police, handcuffed, searched roughly, and shoved in the back of a patrol car. When they got to the police station he was placed under arrest for the murder of a police officer.

Gerry remembered little about the trial. The jury found him not guilty by reason of insanity, and the judge ordered that he be sent to the Lepine Institute. The murder, the trial, those first few months at the Institute, they remained a blur in his memory, distant and unreal, like an old movie or a TV show. Yet they had really happened. He had fired the rifle and killed a policewoman and now had to stay in the Institute.

At first he refused treatment and the doctors left him alone. Then, gradually, the poison of the horrible events drained from his mind. He became less agitated and Corinne visited him more often. Perhaps the visits were responsible, at least in part, for his improvement. After one year, he relented and agreed to meet the therapist. Another year passed, and now he was about to leave the Institute for Nancy's birthday. His eyes closed, and when he reopened them, it was seven o'clock in the morning. Happy birthday, Nancy, your father's coming to the party. And then there would be the private party with Corinne.

Corinne picked him up at ten and they drove to the shopping centre to buy gifts. As they stepped from the car, she kissed him lightly. It was good to be out for a day. He chose a large pink Teddy bear for Nancy. Then they walked hand in hand to the cosmetic counter, where Corinne chose a bottle of toilet water. Gerry paid for the gifts, and they headed home.

The day out was not as exciting as the anticipation. The small apartment was as small as ever. If anything, it looked even smaller and shabbier. Corinne's mother was there for the party and so was the next-door neighbour and one other child, a twelve-year-old girl who lived in the building. Nancy wore a gold birthday hat, blew a whistle, and managed to spread chocolate from the cake all over her face. At first, she was reluctant to come near him, but after a few minutes she overcame her shyness. The Teddy bear was an instant hit.

After the guests left, Nancy fell asleep in the convertible crib and playpen in the corner of the living room. Gerry looked expectantly at Corinne and she responded. They lay together in her bed but failed to reach the height of pleasure he had imagined. He was nervous and clumsy, unable to restrain his impatience. Afterwards they talked until Nancy's cries interrupted the calm. They rose, dressed, and walked to the park. Gerry's first day out was over. When he returned to the Institute that night, he felt a sense of relief. As the day out receded in time, his memory embellished each detail so that his recollection of the day's events surpassed reality.

Corinne and Nancy continued to visit Gerry at the Institute each Sunday, and twice more that year he was allowed out of the Institute. But these visits were equally disappointing. After the second time, his imagination could no longer embellish the encounters. He realized that it was all over between him and Corinne. They had a long talk. Corinne had decided to take her life in hand and had enrolled in a dental hygienist course. She could not live alone forever and would go out with other men. He nodded and said he understood. She promised to keep visiting him.

Shortly thereafter, Corinne married and moved to a house in the suburbs. Her husband was an insurance agent and could afford a nicer home. The visits to the Institute became less frequent. Gerry did not ask for more days out because there was nowhere to go. He wrote Nancy and hoped his letters would be read to her. Whenever possible, a twenty-dollar bill was enclosed. Gerry continued the therapy and devoted himself to the plumbing work assignments. He sent Nancy a present for each birthday, but saw her only three or four times a year.

Two months after Nancy's fifth birthday, Gerry Rousseau was declared cured and released from the Institute. He rented an apartment not unlike the one he had occupied with Corinne years earlier. After a while, he managed to obtain temporary jobs as a plumber on small construction projects. He got in touch with Corinne, but she was not happy to hear from him and his requests to see Nancy were usually refused. On rare occasions she agreed to meet him in a park or shopping centre, and he would spend a short time with his daughter under Corinne's watchful eye. Once they went to a Burger King for lunch. When Corinne insisted on reimbursing him for her hamburger and coffee, they had a fight and he stomped out.

After that incident Corinne refused to meet him, and contact with Nancy was now limited to the occasional phone call. Gerry was upset about this and phoned his therapist at the Institute to find out what he could do. The therapist referred him to the legal aid office, where lawyer Pierrette Fontaine launched proceedings for Gerry to obtain visiting rights every second weekend. Corinne contested the proceedings and asked that he be deprived of all parental authority. Her attorney had advised this would be a preliminary step to an application for permission for her husband to adopt Nancy. The application for visiting rights was set down for trial before me.

"My lord, the plaintiff will present two witnesses. Doctor Bernard Gauthier and himself. I had wished to begin with Doctor Gauthier. However, he has not arrived yet. I believe that he is delayed by traffic. Would you agree to adjourn for several moments until his arrival?"

"Ms. Fontaine," I replied, "you know that there are other parties and attorneys in court today waiting to be heard. I can offer you two alternatives. Proceed immediately or postpone the hearing of your case and I shall begin another."

"I shall proceed immediately. Mr. Gerry Rousseau will testify."

She nodded to her client. He rose, walked to the witness stand, and repeated the oath. Pierrette's questioning was thorough. Gerry explained that his mother had died when he was only five and his father had been the dominant influence in his life. The father, a small contractor who worked for himself, had a violent temper. Gerry feared him and learned to anticipate and avoid his rages and tantrums. Gerry went on to explain how he had left school and drifted into the relationship with Corinne. He described the birth of their child, his futile attempt to run away, and the terrible day he had killed the policewoman. The criminal trial and subsequent imprisonment were glossed over.

"Since I began the therapy," Gerry continued, "I have learned to control my fears. I speak more now. I can tell people how I feel without becoming angry. I tried to tell Corinne how I feel about Nancy. Corinne has married and moved into a nice house, but Nancy is my child and I want to see her. Do you know that when I first got out of Lepine, I phoned Corinne and told her I had a hundred dollars for Nancy. She told me to keep the money, that I needed it more than she did, and she only let me see Nancy a few times. Once we went to Burger King together, Corinne, Nancy, and me. She let me pay for Nancy's meal, but wouldn't let me buy her a coffee. I said what I thought, and she got mad. She said that I couldn't see Nancy again until I learned not to argue. Nancy is my daughter, and I want to see her. That was when I went to the legal aid clinic. I want to see Nancy, I want to see Nancy. I am her father. I . . . "

"The Court will adjourn for fifteen minutes," I interjected. The usher took my black notebook and opened the door. I rose and walked slowly to the office. This was going to be a difficult day. I had read the file before entering the courtroom. Custody fights can be difficult to resolve, and there is always concern for the children who must live with the consequences of the decision, but usually the issues are less stark. This would not be a question of where the child should live, which school to attend, or which parent would be with the child on Christmas Eve. On the surface, the case was about visiting rights, but in fact the physical well-being if not the life of the child and her mother were possibly at risk. If Gerry did not present a physical threat, he should be allowed to see Nancy at regular intervals. But if there was danger, I would have to prohibit all contact, and this would create pressures that Gerry might not be able to withstand. Undoubtedly, the doctors would tell me he was cured, but I, and not they, would have to make this decision. And I knew nothing about Nancy. In custody proceedings, lawyers frequently spend so much time boasting about their client's characters, homes, and leisure facilities, that they forget to describe the child who is the object of the lawsuit.

235

"Should I sue them?"

"What are you talking about?" I asked my secretary.

She continued on into my office, "Did you forget so soon? Remember, I told you yesterday that the transmission on my car was broken and Metro Auto, your former client, refuses to fix it on the guarantee. Well, the fellow who calls you "Your Excellency" called to tell me that the repairs will cost $1,500, the manufacturer is not responsible, the insurance company is broke, and he was very sorry but he won't pay. What should I do? While you solve the problems of the world, can you spare me some advice?"

"First of all, remain calm, and above all, don't return the car they lent you until you have settled matters. Then call the treasurer and tell him "His Excellency" is presiding in a matter of great importance and relies upon him to resolve this small matter of a transmission. If necessary, I'll call him when I have time and patience, which is not now."

"Yes, My Excellency," she said, with an elaborate curtsy and a smile. "Your usher is waiting to lead you back to the courtroom. *Bonne journée*, Your Excellency. I shall report to you at noon."

I waved at her departing figure, picked up my black note-book, and returned to the courtroom.

"How often do you wish to see your daughter?" Pierrette Fontaine asked.

"Every second weekend. I want to be like any other father. She can sleep at my apartment every second weekend. I want to be with my daughter during the Christmas holidays and for a month every summer."

"How large is your apartment?"

"Three and a half rooms. There is a bedroom where I sleep, a kitchen and a living room. Nancy can sleep over on the couch in the living room."

"Do you have a job?"

"Yes."

"What is your weekly salary?"

"Two hundred and fifty dollars."

"Your witness," announced Pierrette Fontaine as she sat down.

Maria Gomez represented Corinne. She was bright, aggressive, and rough around the edges. In a few years, she would mature into an excellent lawyer, but at the moment she lacked the insight and compassion that comes with experience.

"How long have you been working at your present job?"

"Six weeks."

"Isn't that the longest time you have held a job in the last year?" she asked sarcastically.

"Yes, it is," Gerry responded in monotone.

"Why can't you keep a job for more than six weeks?"

"I've tried, but I was not lucky. I do construction work. I'm a plumber, and the building business is not good these days. I was laid off a few times."

"Laid off? or fired?"

"Laid off. It's not easy. I am the first person they lay off. The newest guy on the job is the first to be fired, and . . . "

"Fired? I thought you said you were never fired. That you were laid off. Did you lie?"

"No. I meant to say that the last guy hired is the first laid off. I wasn't fired. I was laid off."

"Are you sure you were laid off and not fired? Remember you are under oath and it is an offence to lie under oath."

"Yes."

"Ms. Gomez," I interjected, "the witness has answered your question. I suggest you move on to the next one."

"Yes, Your Lordship. Mr. Rosseau, would you describe all the jobs you have held since your release from pris — from the Institute?"

Gerry Rousseau spoke for several minutes about his work experience. Since leaving the Institute he had drifted from one construction site to another, doing small jobs. On a few occasions he had collected unemployment insurance and the previous winter he had been unemployed for a stretch of two and a half months. Though several of his employers had re-engaged him a second time when the work was available and some of his jobs had lasted two or three weeks, none had lasted more than six weeks. He hoped his present job would last longer because he was working at a site of a small shopping centre.

Maria Gomez persisted, harping on every detail, seeking the slightest contradictions and magnifying them beyond proportion in an attempt to discredit and provoke the witness. Periodically, my mind would wander off as she repeated answers that she approved, and then continued to explore the minutiae of each building where Rousseau had worked. Perhaps, when this trial was over I would recommend her services as an attorney to represent my secretary against Metro Auto. She would know how to recover the full amount of the repairs to the transmission. The treasurer would fold under her onslaught.

I glanced at the digital clock near the controls for the recording machines; it was twelve-thirty. "The Court will adjourn until two-fifteen," I announced. When I returned to my office, my secretary had gone for lunch. She'd left a note on my desk:

Your Excellency,

My car is still broken. The "Treasurer" said it would be impossible to get money from the manufacturer for me, but he will try to do it for you. Please call him when you have time. He wishes to hear your voice.

Jackie

P.S. I should have bought a Honda!

The afternoon was devoted to completion of the cross-examination of Gerry Rousseau. Maria Gomez used every weapon in her arsenal, but she could not get him to explode. She probed, goaded, and mocked him mercilessly. Pierrette Fontaine objected to the badgering of the witness and I intervened frequently in a futile attempt to lower the heat.

"Ms. Gomez, I think you are being too tough on the witness!"

"Life is tough, Your Lordship. This witness lived a protected life in an institution while my client had to fend for herself and her child. She managed to pull her act together, and she had rearranged her life, married, and found a good, steady job. It wasn't easy. It was tough, and she and I will be tough in protecting Nancy from her father!"

"Ms. Gomez, have you finished your cross-examination?"

"I have two more questions."

"Please continue."

The Court adjourned at twenty to five. It had been a long day. But one thing had been established. Gerry Rousseau had learned to control his temper. He had also been well coached by his attorney to withstand the cross-examination. The trial had been set down for two days, but was obviously going to last longer, and arrangements would have to be made to refer my other case to another judge.

I returned to my office. "By the way," my secretary said, "I have to reply to the last invitation you received for the judges' golf tournament. Will you go?"

"Of course not. You know I don't play golf."

"I know, but I thought you might go for the meal. You can borrow my car . . . if the transmission is fixed by then . . . "

"Do you mean you haven't solved that problem yet?"

"No, and you haven't helped me either!"

"Okay, I guess I'll have to get involved. Please try and reach my friend at Metro Auto."

"Too late," she answered. "He's the treasurer, not the

service manager. Executives come in late and play golf in the afternoon. When I phoned half an hour ago, he was out for the day."

Doctor Gauthier was the first witness the following morning. He described his professional and academic qualifications. He had studied and written an impressive number of articles for psychiatric journals, taught at the university in the faculty of medicine, worked for ten years at the Lepine Institute, and was currently in private practice. There could be no doubting his competence as an expert witness. He had been given access to the Institute's files on Gerry and this study was supplemented by two lengthy interviews and his observation of most of the previous day's court proceedings.

Pierrette Fontaine questioned the witness slowly, allowing him to determine the pace and to elaborate on points he considered important. He referred to the written report in the court record and described the situation in simple terms. Gerry had reacted to the pressures placed upon him by his father, and the birth of his daughter had forced these concerns to the forefront. The pressure had mounted and induced temporary paranoia, manifested in his fear of being killed by Kid Trent. This is what had caused him to run from his home and abandon his child. The shooting of the policewoman had been an involuntary act committed under the delusion associated with the paranoia. During the six months following the killing, all the impulses engendered were gradually dissipated and the danger of recurrence had been successfully combated during the years of therapy that Gerry had undergone at the Institute. Dr. Gauthier and his colleagues at the Institute now considered that Gerry was in remission and could resume his place in society without endangering his family and acquaintances.

I listened to the testimony and simultaneously skimmed through the typewritten report. I would have to be convinced by more than this, however. Doubts gnawed at my mind. Could I grant Gerry the right to be alone with his daughter for the weekend? I appreciated his attachment and love for the child. The saving of small sums from his salary at the Institute and his modest gifts to the child were impressive. But people have been harmed by concerned parents. And he could be capable of abandoning the child again — as he had done six years ago.

"Finally," Doctor Gauthier continued, "my observation of Gerry's behaviour during more than four hours of cross-examination confirms the findings of my colleagues and myself. The pressure placed upon him in the courtroom yesterday is as great as any that he is likely to encounter. He absorbed the pressure and demonstrated his ability to function in situations of extreme stress. I therefore recommend to the Court that Gerry Rousseau be permitted to visit his daughter, Nancy, on a frequent basis, and following the initial visits, that the child visit and sleep over at his apartment on alternate weekends." He faced me directly, bowed slightly, and said, "Naturally, the frequency and timing of these visits are a matter best left for the Court to decide." It was eleven o'clock. I announced a fifteen-minute adjournment before cross-examination and returned to my office. The smell of fresh coffee and a smile on Jackie's face signalled good news. She followed me into my private office carrying a cup.

"I spoke to the treasurer," she said as I sat down behind my desk. "We were eyeball-to-eyeball over the phone and I think he just blinked."

"I suspect that you were vocal chord to vocal chord and the other fellow coughed. What happened?"

"He offered $200, which he said he had obtained as a goodwill gesture from the manufacturer."

"What did you reply?"

"I asked him if Metro Auto intended to show some goodwill as well."

"Good. Did he respond?"

"Well, not at first. He said that he would have to speak to the president because they would be taking the money out of funds allocated for advertising and diverting it to repair costs and direct labour."

"Do you believe this gibberish?"

"Of course not. I told him that I was sure that as treasurer of one of the largest car dealerships in Montreal, he had enough authority to deal personally with matters of this kind. He said that he did, and that the dealership would absorb $200 of the repair cost as well. He wanted to know "His Excellency's" opinion of the combined goodwill gesture of $400 for the repair of the transmission."

"And . . . "

"He will call you personally at twelve-thirty. He said he would round the offer up to $500 if you speak to him."

"I don't know if I feel like speaking to him today. This case I have is getting to me. It's about a fellow who killed a policewoman and . . . "

"Give him life!"

"He was found not guilty by reason of insanity. Now the doctors declare him cured and I have to decide visiting and access rights. Something is bothering me. The child is only six."

"Leave the car matter to me and concentrate on your trial. But just do me one favour. If you decide to render judgement off the Bench, try not to use those long psychiatric expressions that end in 's-i-s,' like psychosis, neurosis, and halitosis. No one understands or can spell them, and remember, you only have to listen, decide, and talk. I have to type the judgment and spell all those words correctly."

Her instinct was right. I had to listen to the experts, but I would have to find a clue to the solution in the testimony of Gerry and Corinne. The doctor had expressed an opinion based on certain facts. I would have to concentrate on all the facts, but perhaps there were others the doctor had not considered.

Not surprisingly, Maria Gomez had prepared for the cross-examination. Several thick textbooks and articles were piled on the counsel table in front of her. She began by asking the doctor to define certain psychological terms: psychotic, narcissistic, paranoid, neurotic.

She led the witness through a lengthy description of various mental conditions and tried to make him define Gerry's condition. The doctor resisted and continued to assert that each person has many different personality traits and that the presence of one or more of these traits does not necessarily lead to the conclusion that the individual must be described as possessing a defined condition and then have all the textbook attributes of that condition ascribed to him. When she was unable to succeed in this line of questioning, she began to explore the difference between the words "cured" and "remission."

"Doctor, would you say that Gerald Rousseau has been cured?"

"I would prefer to say that he is in remission."

"Does that mean the same thing as cured?"

"Not exactly."

"Would a person in remission be likely to commit the act which characterized the original condition, such as cause harm to someone without provocation or justification?"

"It's not likely."

"Is it possible?"

"Everything is possible. Yes, it is possible."

"Is it more possible in the case of Gerry Rousseau than in the case of someone such as me or His Lordship?"

"I cannot say. I do believe that as a result of the therapy, Gerry Rousseau is now in remission and can be considered within the range of normality. That means he is no more or less likely to commit such an act than any other individual."

"But he did in the past, did he not?"

"Yes, I am so informed."

She pressed on. "Is there a possibility that you are wrong in your assessment?"

"Yes, there is always a possibility, but I am expressing an opinion on the basis of my twenty-five years of experience. I believe my opinion is correct. Moreover, my opinion is confirmed by those of my former colleagues at the Lepine Institute."

"Were you aware of their opinion before you formed your own opinion?"

"Yes, I was. I had access to the file before I met Gerry Rousseau, and in fact, read the file before our first meeting."

"So you did not form an opinion of your own. You merely confirmed their opinion?"

"I would not put it that way. I reached an opinion based on my total findings, which included the file and opinions of others."

"Do you ever disagree with the opinion of other psychiatrists?"

"Yes. That occurs in every profession, including law, I understand."

"Is it possible that another psychiatrist would disagree with your opinion in this case?"

"Everything is possible, but it is unlikely."

"Would you say that an unprovoked attack and killing of a police officer is also possible but unlikely?"

"Yes, I guess so."

"Is that a guess or an opinion?"

"I only give opinions within my field of competence. I must leave it to others to determine the frequency or likelihood of unprovoked attacks on policemen and women in general."

This was starting to get out of hand. I looked at Maria and motioned to her to calm down. She acknowledged my gesture with a slight nod and went on to another subject.

"Doctor, did you interview Nancy?"

"No."

"Don't you think it is important that you see the child before recommending to this Court that her father, who has just been released from a mental institution after committing a homicide, be granted visiting rights?"

"No, I did not believe that her personality and ability to cope was an issue in this case. I was asked to limit my examination to the personality of Mr. Rousseau and I would have made the same recommendation regardless of the age or personality of the child."

"What if she detests or fears her father? What would you say if she refused to see him?"

"My opinion is an opinion of the normality of Gerry Rousseau and whether he constitutes a danger to other people. I have told you my opinion. As far as the child is concerned, her reaction would have to be assessed by others. That was not my role in this matter."

"So you really know nothing about Nancy, other than what you have heard about her from Gerry Rousseau and in this courtroom?"

"Yes."

"And still you feel able to express a professional opinion that it is in her best interest to see her biological father and visit and sleep at his house?"

"I expressed my opinion as to whether or not Gerry Rousseau represents a danger to other people. My answer is no. I express no opinion as to the mental state or condition of Nancy, other than to tell you that her father wants to see her and considers her a bright, healthy child."

"Doctor, her father has testified. Please limit your remarks to what you know personally."

"Ms. Gomez," I interjected. "You asked the question and the witness answered. I suggest you withhold your comments on his testimony until the argument stage."

"Yes, my lord, no further questions of this witness."

I looked at Doctor Gauthier and asked, "Doctor, is there any possibility of danger to Nancy if I authorize visiting rights in favour of her father?"

"Yes, Your Honour, there is always some risk. There is a risk of danger to her at home, at school, and elsewhere. The threat to her welfare is no greater in the presence of her father than elsewhere."

"Will you rest easily tonight if I accept and act on your opinion?"

"Yes."

"Would you give me the same answer if Nancy were your grandchild or niece?"

He hesitated before answering.

"Yes, your Honour. I mean, Your Lordship."

"Thank you."

Pierrette Fontaine rose and announced: "No further witnesses. The proof of plaintiff is closed."

"Thank you," I responded. "It is now twelve-thirty. The proof of the defendant will commence at two-fifteen. The Court is adjourned until that time."

As I entered my office, my secretary was speaking on the phone. She gestured to me and mouthed the words "The treasurer." I nodded in comprehension and entered my private office. "His Lordship has just returned from court," I could hear her say. "He will speak to you now."

I lifted the receiver and said, "Hello, hello, how nice to hear from you. I am flattered that you are able to find the time to attend to this very trivial matter of my secretary's transmission."

"Oh no, Your Excellency," he replied. "Every customer is important to us at the Metro Auto. Have you heard the good news?"

"No, have you been awarded another franchise? Did the manufacturer recall the last recall?"

"Do not joke with me, Your Excellency. I am referring to you secretary's automobile. I have convinced the manufacturer to participate in our goodwill gesture, and the manufacturer and Metro Auto are prepared to contribute a total of $500 towards the cost of a new transmission. What do you say now?"

"That is indeed good news, Mr. Treasurer. But I am not as skilled as you in mathematics. In my simple calculation, it would appear that a large automobile manufacturer and Metro Auto, the largest dealer in this area, will each contribute $250, while my poor secretary, an underpaid civil servant, must contribute $1,000. Considering that the repairs were to be covered by an insurance policy, I find that incomprehensible."

"Your Excellency, you are right. Alas, I cannot do anything. I am only a small dealer who must follow instructions from the manufacturer."

"You are the person who sold her the insurance policy and assured her that there would never be a problem, are you not?"

"Sir, you are right again. I shall once again urge her case before the manufacturer. I shall call the customer relations officer for the Eastern region, impress him with the seriousness of the matter, and then I shall be able to obtain a better settlement for the transmission. Your Excellency, do not worry. We take care of our people."

"Thank you, Treasurer. As always, it is a pleasure dealing with you. Please give my regards to the president, who is undoubtedly aware of this matter."

"Most surely. Good day."

My secretary appeared at the door the moment I set down the receiver. "Well, what did he say? Will they pay?"

"Not yet," I replied. "First he must speak to the eastern region customer relations officer. Don't worry, he'll come through with more money for you. Give him time."

Corinne was the sole witness for the defence. Maria tried to guide her through her testimony, but this was not feasible. It was apparent that she had reviewed the facts in her head many times and was determined to tell her story in her own way. There was no significant difference between her version of the early events and that of Gerry. He had encouraged her to go out with other men and to remake her life. She was proud of her new career as a dental hygienist and spoke at length of the dental clinic where she worked.

When she described her husband's relationship with Nancy, the muscles of her face tightened. She had built a new family and career and would fight to preserve them from outside intrusion. Gerry was an intruder, a disruptive influence in the life of his child that she would not tolerate. As she came to the most recent period following Gerry's discharge from the Institute, she retrieved a notebook from her handbag and referred to it for dates and other details. She had kept a diary of every meeting, phone call, and note involving Gerry. Nancy was her child, and she alone would determine who could see her and when. She spoke for one hour without stopping. When she concluded, the Court adjourned for a brief period.

My secretary was typing away and pretended to ignore my presence. I knew immediately that something was happening, but two can play that game. I ignored her, entered my office, and glanced at some of the unsolicited newspapers that arrive daily from professional, government, and other organizations. As I thumbed through the catalogue of a legal publisher, the noise in the outer office stopped. Jackie entered my office and said, "I'm sorry. I was so engrossed in your last judgment that I didn't see you come in. How is the case going?"

"Not easy. This one is going to be hard to decide. The proof is almost concluded and I haven't found the cornerstone upon which to build a decision. I see both parents' point of view, and as usual they are both right. I can't decide if there is any danger to the child. The mother is trying to rewrite history. It's obvious that she regrets that her husband is not Nancy's father and would like to make some kind of substitution. That lady is tough. Tougher than her lawyer, who is no shrinking violet. I'll keep listening and hope for some insight. What's happening here?"

"The president of Metro Auto called you."

"Did you leave a message in my name?"

"No, don't get mad. He probably just phoned to invite you for lunch and sell you a car. Business is bad and you're an easy mark."

"No, he's been speaking to the treasurer. The president doesn't want to speak to me. He phoned when it was likely I would be out. He just wants to take credit for what's going to happen. The Treasurer will call before the end of the day and make a new offer. Unless I'm wrong, he will offer to pay the full amount of the repairs."

"It's time for you to return to court."

The cross-examination of Corinne was uneventful. It was hard not to respect what she had accomplished. Even though Pierrette believed in her case, she had neither the desire nor the stomach to embark on a lengthy interrogation. She asked a few perfunctory questions and sat down.

"Would you mind answering one or two additional questions?" I asked.

"No, Your Honour."

"Could you please tell me a little about Nancy? Does she have friends, does she attend school, is she in good health, does she know about the terrible incident that occurred when she was a few days old?"

The expression on Corinne's face softened. "Nancy is a bright, lovely child. I have some pictures with me. May I show them to you?"

"Yes, of course."

She handed me several photographs from her handbag. "She is in kindergarten and she loves school. I take her to her class every morning. She only goes for half-days. A neighbour brings her to my mother's home each afternoon and my husband picks her up on his way home from the office. We work things out very well. She knows about her father. He told her himself. He didn't tell her everything, but she knows that he accidentally killed a policewoman and was in the hospital for a long time. I didn't want him to tell her, but he insisted. That is one of the reasons I don't want him to see Nancy. She is too young to hear these things. She is too young to see her father. He should wait a few years. First he must prove that he has changed."

"If I decide that Mr. Rousseau should have regular visiting privileges, what do you think would be an appropriate way to handle the arrangements?"

"I want him to write me and see her only when it is convenient for me, and I want to be present all the time. I won't trust my child with him. He calls too often. Here, here is my notebook. You heard my testimony but you can read it for yourself. I am not hiding anything. You'll see how often he calls."

"Thank you. You may sit down beside your attorney."

The concluding arguments were predictable. Pierrette Fontaine made an emotional plea on behalf of her client. He had spent five years at the Lepine Institute, clung to his relationship with Nancy, undergone therapy, and managed to be cured. The psychiatric evidence was uncontradicted, Gerry did not represent any danger to his daughter, and was entitled to see her on a regular basis.

Maria Gomez feigned indignation. Her client had suffered for years as a single parent, reorganized her life, married, and started again, and was being dragged down by this man who had run away from his responsibilities as a father, killed a policewoman, and was an unfit father. She considered the medical testimony to be inconclusive. She ended, "Life is tough. My client had the strength of character to survive and overcome the problems created by the plaintiff. She has raised and defended her child and is entitled to continue to make all decisions in the child's interest. The plaintiff caused the death of a policewoman. We can forgive him but we cannot trust him. Corinne cannot trust him, Nancy cannot trust him, and the Court must not do so."

"Judgment will be rendered at nine-thirty tomorrow morning," I announced. "The Court is adjourned."

This was going to be a difficult night, but there was no point in postponing the decision. I knew as much as I would ever know about this case. If I waited, I would probably forget something.

My secretary was waiting for me. This time she beamed, unable to contain herself. "The treasurer called again. He said he could not understand how it happened, but the president called him and they discussed the transmission on my car. They are now ready to pay $1,000. The manufacturer will pay $500, Metro Auto will pay $500, and I must pay $500. He thought you would be pleased. He said they have met me more than halfway."

"Wonderful! If a man were drowning a hundred feet from shore, they would throw him a sixty-five-foot rope and say they met him more than halfway. I'm sorry. The case I just heard is bothering me. I suggest you phone the Treasurer and accept his offer."

"I did, thank you for the advice. Now I can lend you my car for the golf tournament. It's not much as a car, but it will look like one awfully impressive golf cart."

I spent a restless night wavering back and forth in my mind. Corinne had demonstrated strength and character when she had turned her back on the past, acquired a profession, and established her family. She had fought for and earned the right to live with her husband and Nancy, undisturbed by intrusions from the past. But neither Corinne nor I could erase the past completely.

Gerry was Nancy's father. That was a fact that would not change. Undoubtedly, Nancy would thrive under her mother's care, but this was not a trial of Corinne's competence as a mother; it was not a custody dispute. The only issue here was occasional visits by Gerry and whether they constituted a danger to Nancy or Corinne.

By morning, I had concluded that Gerry was not dangerous. The psychiatric testimony was credible. Gerry had held up well under the stress of the trial, and the child was healthy both physically and emotionally, and able to deal with the situation. My final doubts were resolved when I read Corinne's diary. Her record of events was dispassionate; she was not afraid. She had received Gerry without fear in her home and bed during his leave from the Institute. She knew Gerry better than anyone else in the world and was not afraid. Usually a parent is granted visiting rights every second weekend, but this case was unusual and the past had to be acknowledged. The visits would have to be less frequent, but Gerry was entitled to see his daughter.

> The Court confirms that the Defendant shall continue to have sole custody of her daughter, Nancy. However, the Plaintiff will have the right to visit his daughter every third Sunday, from ten o'clock in the morning until four in the afternoon. This access is less than usually granted, but the past circumstances are exceptional. The visits will be unsupervised because there is no danger to the child. This finding is based on the observations made during this two-day trial, the records of the Lepine Institute, the testimony of the psychiatrist, and most of all the perception of the Defendant who indicated no fear whatsoever when she described the Plaintiff in her

diary which she voluntarily filed in the court record. Nor was she fearful of receiving the Plaintiff in her home and arms two years after the accident. The Court is adjourned.

Gerry began to cry. Corinne nodded her head up and down slowly. I looked on impassively for several seconds before leaving the courtroom. Maria was right. *Life is tough!*

Afterword: Review by the Critics

Justice is the ideal that courts try to attain by applying law and judicial experience to particular facts and circumstances. Although the ideal result is not always achieved, the system works surprisingly well. The genius of the law and the accumulated wisdom, which we call precedent, put forward by lawyers and sifted and weighed by judges, provide a liveable, workable, and reasonable solution to most problems. But judges are fallible, and reason and conscience may diverge. Since some problems are insoluble, some results undesired, and some consequences unintended, a judgment may leave the judge, the parties, and even the witnesses with a profound sense of inadequacy and incomprehension. But failure, uncomfortable situations, and unhappy endings are part of both theatre and life. Recognition of this reality is not a denial of the effectiveness and justness of the system, but rather an incentive to legislators, judges, lawyers, and philosophers of law to seek and strive for a better world.

The losing party who believes a judgment is wrong may request that the Court of Appeal review the trial record, correct major errors, and revise the judgment of the judge who presided at the trial. This process is initiated by filing a document that contains a brief outline of the errors attributed to the trial judge and the corrections suggested. The decision of the three or more judges who hear the appeal is based on the written record of what transpired in the lower court and the written and oral submissions of the attorneys. In exceptional circumstances, witnesses may be heard, and new documents may be examined at this stage.

Courts of Appeal are frequently presented with problems that require old legal precedents to be reinterpreted and new guidelines and principles to be established in response to changing circumstances and new situations. They chart the path where the law should develop and seek to ensure that they and their colleagues present a united front so that clear direction can be given to the lower courts. They are aware that inevitably some judgments of the lower courts will be overruled and that the judges of those courts often have a fierce sense of pride and forget the old adage, "Occasionally overruled but never upset."

The task of an appellate judge is therefore not easy. What's more, the workload is heavy and the flow of reading material endless. Friends on the Appeal Court have complained to me that they have little time to read for pleasure and that the occasional short novel is a rare distraction and delight. Justice Tannenbaum recounts how a senior colleague took him aside one day and advised, "Remember Louis, if they should ever offer to elevate you to the Court of Appeal, *it's the same salary!*"

Some judgments cannot be appealed because the amount at issue is below the established financial threshold. Unsuccessful parties to lawsuits where a lesser amount is involved must find other ways to express their dissatisfaction with a decision.

Judge Mendelson was once presiding in small claims court, where he heard a claim for $760. The damages occurred when the plaintiff's automobile was towed from a shopping centre where it had been parked illegally. When the action was dismissed, the plaintiff threatened, "Your Honour, I don't like that judgment. I am going to call a policeman!"

Some appeals are launched to obtain additional time for the losing party and are ultimately settled or abandoned. Urgent matters can be heard within six months; others are heard and decided within two years of the first judgment. Roughly two-thirds of the appeals heard are dismissed.

As a courtesy, a copy of the Inscription in Appeal is always forwarded to the "learned trial judge who erred." My old friend Justice Mackay suggested that a judge who receives notice of an appeal from one of his judgments should refrain from reading it. Why read a lengthy catalogue of attributed errors and risk discouragement? If the appeal is withdrawn, the effort is fruitless. If it proceeds, the judgment of the Court of Appeal will contain a detailed analysis of the first judgment. Sage advice, well followed.

After an arduous day of questioning and testimony by witnesses, D and K presented their closing arguments. I listened intently, made up my mind, and gave my judgment. I then left the courtroom and promptly forgot about the case. Three weeks later K inscribed in appeal against my judgment. Following Justice Mackay's advice, I did not read the copy of the inscription delivered to my office but upon leaving the palace for the day, I encountered K standing in front of the building.

"That was an awfully good judgment that you gave in the case D and I pleaded before you a few weeks ago," he remarked. "We had been negotiating all week. Without even knowing our positions, you managed to come down the middle. Really good."

"Well," I said, "if the judgment was so good, why did you go to appeal?"

"Ah, clients. They're never satisfied."

Two months later K's partner was pleading a similar matter involving other parties. At the conclusion of her presentation, she submitted as authority and as an appropriate precedent my judgment, which K had appealed.

"I am always in complete agreement with myself," I stated, "but you must be aware of the fact that your partner who pleaded that case has appealed to the Court of Appeal to revise my judgment because I erred in law."

"I know," she responded, "but he is not serious about the appeal. Please follow the line of thought in your first judgment."

I did.

Eighteen months later, I met K at a bar meeting. He informed me that the appeal had been withdrawn.

While sitting in the Administrative Division, I was once presented with a motion for Declaratory Judgment (that is, an application for a judge's interpretation of a law, contract, or document required to solve a genuine problem). I read the file rapidly and suggested to the attorneys that the procedure was not available in the circumstances of their case and that I lacked jurisdiction to hear them.

The attorneys, Ron Martin and Robert Bochatz, prevailed upon me to hear the matter despite my reservations and undertook not to raise the question of jurisdiction. Since the Court roll for that day was light, I acquiesced.

Later that day, when I rendered judgment against Bochatz's client, I mentioned the fact that although my jurisdiction was questionable, both attorneys had consented to the use of the procedure.

Two weeks later, Bochatz inscribed in appeal against the judgment. The inscription announced that:

The learned trial judge lacked jurisdiction and erred in arrogating to himself a jurisdiction he did not possess under the provisions of the law respecting declaratory judgments.

That was too much. I was determined to put Bochatz in his place at the appropriate moment. When he came to see me on a totally unrelated matter almost a year later, I broached the subject.

"Bochatz, I don't like to carry grudges against lawyers. My mind gets cluttered. So I shall say what I think. You're a scoundrel."

"What's wrong?" asked Bochatz.

"Do you remember that application for declaratory judgment with Ron Martin? You asked me to do you a favour and hear the application despite my reservations about jurisdiction. You undertook not to invoke that ground, and then appealed on the ground that I lacked jurisdiction!"

"I would never do such a thing!" he replied.

"Don't tell me that. I received a copy of the Inscription in Appeal and that is the first ground raised. I don't mind if you question the reasons for the judgment — but the jurisdiction?"

"I didn't know you received copies of the Inscription. I didn't question your jurisdiction. I agreed not to do so. You must have made a mistake."

As I picked up the phone to ask my secretary to bring in the Inscription, there was a knock at the door of my office. Before I could respond, my secretary entered, carrying a document. As usual, she had either read my mind or listened at the door.

"I thought you might wish to see this Inscription in Appeal," she commented. She then managed to turn slowly, smile at me, scowl at Bochatz, and leave in one fluid motion. I thrust the document into his hands.

"Here, read for yourself and look at the signature."

Bochatz studied the document intently for a few minutes. He then looked up innocently and said, "I admit it's my signature, but did you notice the typing?"

"No, what are you talking about?"

Bochatz beamed. "That's not my secretary's typing. Someone else in the office must have typed the Inscription while I was out of the office and I obviously signed without reading it. Don't worry. I won't raise the matter in my oral presentation to the Court of Appeal."

Repressing a few less than judicious thoughts, I waved him out with a smile. "Get out of here, you scoundrel!"

No matter the division where a judge is assigned, he or she is always sitting in the court of public opinion. Judgments that attract comment by the media and the public may be given erroneous or irrelevant reports, but the impact and impression remain.

On one occasion, I was asked to order the government to compensate the victim of a defective vaccine. The plaintiff had been embroiled in litigation for eighteen years and the Supreme Court, which had dismissed the claim, simultaneously suggested that the government adopt a special law to authorize compensation. The law was passed but the compensation was never paid.

The attorneys for the government argued that I lacked jurisdiction, and in any event, the Minister had undertaken to make the payment. I requested that the letter from the Minister be given to me and read it aloud to the assembled audience and reporters. I then announced that I had every confidence that the Minister would respect his undertaking and postponed the hearing for thirty days. The headlines on the following day read, variously:

JUDGE REFUSES TO ORDER PAYMENT BY MINISTER
JUDGE ORDERS MINISTER TO PAY
JUDGE REFUSES TO HEAR VACCINE CASE

Despite the contradictory headlines, each newspaper carried a lengthy history of the case. The public may have been confused about my order, but the attorneys for the government understood perfectly. Twenty-nine days later I received a copy of a letter the government had sent the victim, together with a photocopy of the enclosed settlement cheque. Reporters who called my secretary the next day were informed, "The judge does not comment on cases before him. You should contact the attorneys for the parties."

When one slaughterhouse was creating problems by emitting odours in violation of zoning restrictions, the neighbours clamoured for action by the city. Previously, the offender had been fined $25 for each infraction. When this proved ineffectual, the City obtained an injunction to prevent the operations from continuing. When the firm failed to respect this order, I found it to be in contempt of court and fined it a "nominal" $10,000. In the body of the judgment, I announced that while the owner had been given the benefit of the doubt this time, he would face imprisonment should further violations occur. The press reported the judgment prominently. The next morning, I was informed that the "Court of Appeal" that meets each morning for breakfast at the Snowdon Deli agreed I had correctly assessed the situation and "fixed the butcher." Mother called that afternoon to express her pride at my accomplishment. The ladies at the golf club felt it was time someone dealt with that arrogant young man, who lands his private helicopter on the field near the golf club and disrupts their games.

Once a judgment is rendered, the judge loses contact with the parties and rarely hears the ultimate result. Did the child continue to live with his mother? Was the labour dispute resolved? Did the accused revert to criminal activity? Was the award paid by the defendant? *Was I right?* He retains the lifeless written judgment, memories, an anecdote or two, and some unanswered questions and doubts.

The judge does derive satisfaction, however, from reading a decision of the Court of Appeal which confirms and quotes at length from the original judgment. Perhaps the only greater pleasure is being overruled by the Court of Appeal and subsequently reinstated by the Supreme Court.

Judgments are also subject to the scrutiny of the legal community. Journals containing important recent judgments are published regularly. The best are reviewed in legal periodicals, submitted as authority in other cases, and quoted by lawyers and judges alike.

One of my first judgments achieved this treatment. Contrary to the terms of its lease, a waffle and crêpe restaurant had closed its business. The issue was whether the Court could oblige the operator to reopen and operate an unprofitable business. Dubbed "The Pancake Judgment," the decision was mentioned at several seminars and reviewed in several legal publications, including a collection of judgments in the field of obligations published at a university law school. Most of the judgments in the collection were in French, only two were in the English language. I wrote to the author of the other English-language judgment:

> I note that of the 96 judgments published in the collection, 94 are in the language of Molière and two are in the language of Shakespeare. It would appear that the

future of English-language jurisprudence in this field is in the hands of you, me, and Shakespeare.

Seven years have elapsed since I was formally presented to my new colleagues by "the judge." I reread and now understand his words:

A judge must be like a plant growing in the desert, dependent solely on its own resources, impervious to the hostile conditions which surround it — absence of moisture, excessive heat and cutting sandstorms. So, too, must a judge ignore the ephemeral plaudits of the populace and the media whenever the decision meets with popular approval. So must he also close his ears to carping criticism and ignore thinly veiled hostility when a decision, sound in law though it may be, is greeted with dissonance. It is not an easy row to hoe: to refuse to play to the gallery and bow to public prejudices, however widely held they may be at the time; to be true to one's oath and render justice without the intervention of mischievous passion; to set aside one's own prejudices and decide each case solely on the basis of law and pure reason. But that is the ideal to which a judge must adhere.

I have returned to my origins in this old quarter of the city. During the 1890s my ancestors landed in the port of Montreal and trekked up The Main to find lodging. My grandfather opened a clothing store at the corner of Craig Street and The Main, less than a hundred yards from the Palais de justice. My grandfather's store is now closed and Governor Craig has suffered the indignity of seeing the name of his street changed to St. Antoine. But The Main is still The Main.

My reminiscing is interrupted as Jackie bursts into my office.

"Why didn't you tell me?"

"Tell you what?" I ask innocently.

"What, what? Tell me you bought me a computer."

"I wanted to surprise you."

"Surprise me? You almost scared me to death. You said you would never spend your judge's allowance to buy me a computer and would wait for the administration to do it. You know what happened last year when you wrote the Chief Justice. He told you to be patient and pray . . . "

"My prayers weren't answered, and I got fed up with waiting for the government to get off their austerity, so I bought one for you."

"Well, you could have told me. The boxes were just delivered, and I almost sent them away before I looked at the label. They were for me, so I opened them."

"And do you like what you found?" I asked.

"Yes, it's a beautiful computer, the newest model, with a colour monitor," she answered, " — a 'Rolls-Royess.'

"Royce, you mean."

"Yes, a 'Rolls-Royess'. . . . But, *Monsieur le juge*, there is one small problem. I must have a table and a new electrical outlet for the computer, and Rocket said there's no money in his budget and no tables in his warehouse."

"Should I understand there is no place to park the 'Rolls-Royess?'" I asked.

"Oui, *Monsieur le juge*. What can we do?"

"First, we must set the scene. Put the kettle and the coffee machine on top of the filing cabinets, park the 'Rolls-Royess' on top of the refrigerator, leave the boxes on the floor, near the door, and get Rocket on the phone for me."

Jackie dialled his local and handed me the receiver.

"*Bonjour*, Hubert," I said breezily.

"*Bonjour, Monsieur le juge*," he responded.

"And how are things at the Maintenance these days?" I asked.

"Very difficult. These are times of recession, and we must tighten our neckties."

"Belts."

"Yes, belts. Nonetheless, we are always at the service of the judiciary, within the limits of budgetary restrictions of course."

"Of course. Hubert, I have this slight problem of parking a 'Rolls-Royess' . . . "

"A what?"

"A rather small 'Rolls-Royess,' and I wondered if you could find the time to drop by my office to discuss this matter."

"But, *Monsieur le juge*, the insurance, and the garage . . ."

"Hubert, I have every confidence you will solve my little problem. Please join me for coffee."

"*Monsieur le juge*, it is my pleasure to be of service."

"Thank you." I replaced the receiver and, turning to Jackie, asked, "Do you remember the last time you plugged the kettle into the wall while the coffee machine, the typewriter, and all the other office equipment were being used?"

"But yes! We blew a fuse and the lights went out."

"That would not be such a bad thing to happen while we entertain Hubert Rocket Racine."

"And then he might install new outlets for the computer?"

"Jackie, I am amazed at how devious you have become. We will solve our little problem, and tomorrow we will enter the computer era."

And so another day begins . . . backstage at the palace!